"After utilizing toolkits from The Art
threats within my organization to whi
my team's knowledge as a competitive advant
systems that save time and energy."

"As a new Chief Technology Officer, I was feeling unprepared and inadequate to be successful in my role. I ordered an IT toolkit Sunday night and was prepared Monday morning to shed light on areas of improvement within my organization. I no longer felt overwhelmed and intimidated, I was excited to share what I had learned."

"I used the questionnaires to interview members of my team. I never knew how many insights we could produce collectively with our internal knowledge."

"I usually work until at least 8pm on weeknights. The Art of Service questionnaire saved me so much time and worry that Thursday night I attended my son's soccer game without sacrificing my professional obligations."

"After purchasing The Art of Service toolkit, I was able to identify areas where my company was not in compliance that could have put my job at risk. I looked like a hero when I proactively educated my team on the risks and presented a solid solution."

"I spent months shopping for an external consultant before realizing that The Art of Service would allow my team to consult themselves! Not only did we save time not catching a consultant up to speed, we were able to keep our company information and industry secrets confidential."

"Everyday there are new regulations and processes in my industry. The Art of Service toolkit has kept me ahead by using AI technology to constantly update the toolkits and address emerging needs."

"I customized The Art of Service toolkit to focus specifically on the concerns of my role and industry. I didn't have to waste time with a generic self-help book that wasn't tailored to my exact situation."

"Many of our competitors have asked us about our secret sauce. When I tell them it's the knowledge we have in-house, they never believe me. Little do they know The Art of Service toolkits are working behind the scenes."

"One of my friends hired a consultant who used the knowledge gained working with his company to advise their competitor. Talk about a competitive disadvantage! The Art of Service allowed us to keep our knowledge from walking out the door along with a huge portion of our budget in consulting fees."

"Honestly, I didn't know what I didn't know. Before purchasing The Art of Service, I didn't realize how many areas of my business needed to be refreshed and improved. I am so relieved The Art of Service was there to highlight our blind spots."

"Before The Art of Service, I waited eagerly for consulting company reports to come out each month. These reports kept us up to speed but provided little value because they put our competitors on the same playing field. With The Art of Service, we have uncovered unique insights to drive our business forward."

"Instead of investing extensive resources into an external consultant, we can spend more of our budget towards pursuing our company goals and objectives...while also spending a little more on corporate holiday parties."

"The risk of our competitors getting ahead has been mitigated because The Art of Service has provided us with a 360-degree view of threats within our organization before they even arise."

GHG Emissions Accounting
Complete Self-Assessment Guide

https://theartofservice.com
support@theartofservice.com

Table of Contents

About The Art of Service

The Art of Service, Business Process Architects since 2000, is dedicated to helping stakeholders achieve excellence.

Defining, designing, creating, and implementing a process to solve a stakeholders challenge or meet an objective is the most valuable role… In EVERY group, company, organization and department.

Unless you're talking a one-time, single-use project, there should be a process. Whether that process is managed and implemented by humans, AI, or a combination of the two, it needs to be designed by someone with a complex enough perspective to ask the right questions.

Someone capable of asking the right questions and step back and say, 'What are we really trying to accomplish here? And is there a different way to look at it?'

With The Art of Service's Self-Assessments, we empower people who can do just that — whether their title is marketer, entrepreneur, manager, salesperson, consultant, Business Process Manager, executive assistant, IT Manager, CIO etc... —they are the people who rule the future. They are people who watch the process as it happens, and ask the right questions to make the process work better.

Contact us when you need any support with this Self-Assessment and any help with templates, blue-prints and examples of standard documents you might need:

https://theartofservice.com
support@theartofservice.com

Included Resources - how to access

Included with your purchase of the book is the GHG Emissions

Accounting Self-Assessment Spreadsheet Dashboard which contains all questions and Self-Assessment areas and auto-generates insights, graphs, and project RACI planning - all with examples to get you started right away.

How? Simply send an email to
access@theartofservice.com
with this books' title in the subject to get the GHG Emissions Accounting Self Assessment Tool right away.

The auto reply will guide you further, you will then receive the following contents with New and Updated specific criteria:

- The latest quick edition of the book in PDF

- The latest complete edition of the book in PDF, which criteria correspond to the criteria in...

- The Self-Assessment Excel Dashboard, and...

- Example pre-filled Self-Assessment Excel Dashboard to get familiar with results generation

- In-depth specific Checklists covering the topic

- Project management checklists and templates to assist with implementation

INCLUDES LIFETIME SELF ASSESSMENT UPDATES

Every self assessment comes with Lifetime Updates and Lifetime Free Updated Books. Lifetime Updates is an industry-first feature which allows you to receive verified self assessment updates, ensuring you always have the most accurate information at your fingertips.

Get it now- you will be glad you did - do it now, before you forget.

Send an email to **access@theartofservice.com** with this books' title in the subject to get the GHG Emissions Accounting Self Assessment Tool right away.

Purpose of this Self-Assessment

This Self-Assessment has been developed to improve understanding of the requirements and elements of GHG Emissions Accounting, based on best practices and standards in business process architecture, design and quality management.

It is designed to allow for a rapid Self-Assessment to determine how closely existing management practices and procedures correspond to the elements of the Self-Assessment.

The criteria of requirements and elements of GHG Emissions Accounting have been rephrased in the format of a Self-Assessment questionnaire, with a seven-criterion scoring system, as explained in this document.

In this format, even with limited background knowledge of GHG Emissions Accounting, a manager can quickly review existing operations to determine how they measure up to the standards. This in turn can serve as the starting point of a 'gap analysis' to identify management tools or system elements that might usefully be implemented in the organization to help improve overall performance.

How to use the Self-Assessment

On the following pages are a series of questions to identify to what extent your GHG Emissions Accounting initiative is complete in comparison to the requirements set in standards.

To facilitate answering the questions, there is a space in front of each question to enter a score on a scale of '1' to '5'.

1 Strongly Disagree

2 Disagree

3 Neutral

4 Agree

5 Strongly Agree

Read the question and rate it with the following in front of mind:

'In my belief,
the answer to this question is clearly defined'.

There are two ways in which you can choose to interpret this statement;

1. how aware are you that the answer to the question is clearly defined
2. for more in-depth analysis you can choose to gather evidence and confirm the answer to the question. This obviously will take more time, most Self-Assessment users opt for the first way to interpret the question and dig deeper later on based on the outcome of the overall Self-Assessment.

A score of '1' would mean that the answer is not clear at all, where a '5' would mean the answer is crystal clear and defined. Leave emtpy when the question is not applicable or you don't want to answer it, you can skip it without affecting your score. Write your score in the space provided.

After you have responded to all the appropriate statements in each section, compute your average score for that section, using the formula provided, and round to the nearest tenth. Then transfer to the corresponding spoke in the GHG Emissions Accounting Scorecard on the second next page of the Self-Assessment.

Your completed GHG Emissions Accounting Scorecard will give you a clear presentation of which GHG Emissions Accounting areas need attention.

GHG Emissions Accounting Scorecard Example

Example of how the finalized Scorecard can look like:

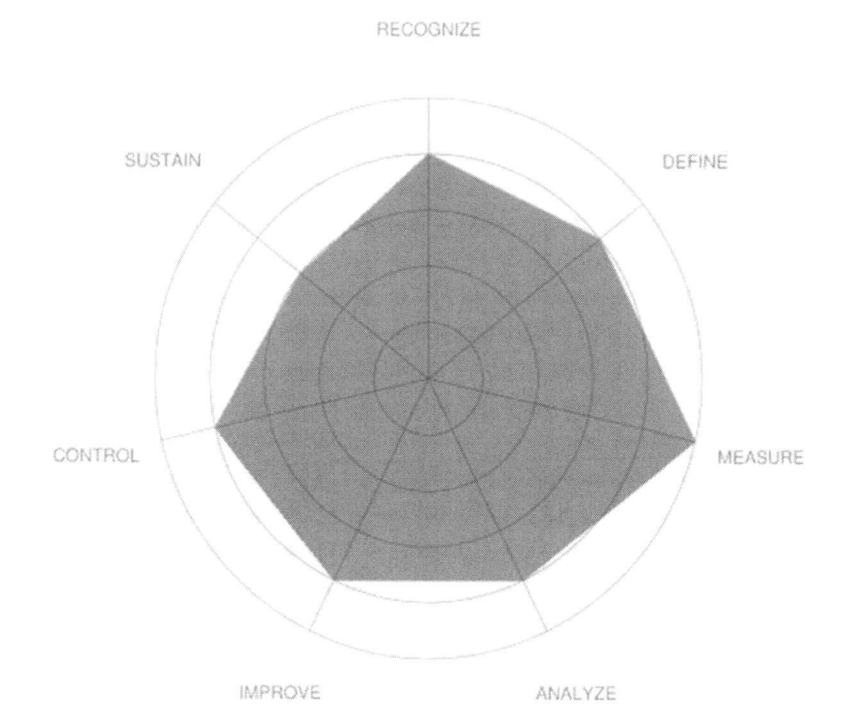

GHG Emissions Accounting Scorecard

Your Scores:

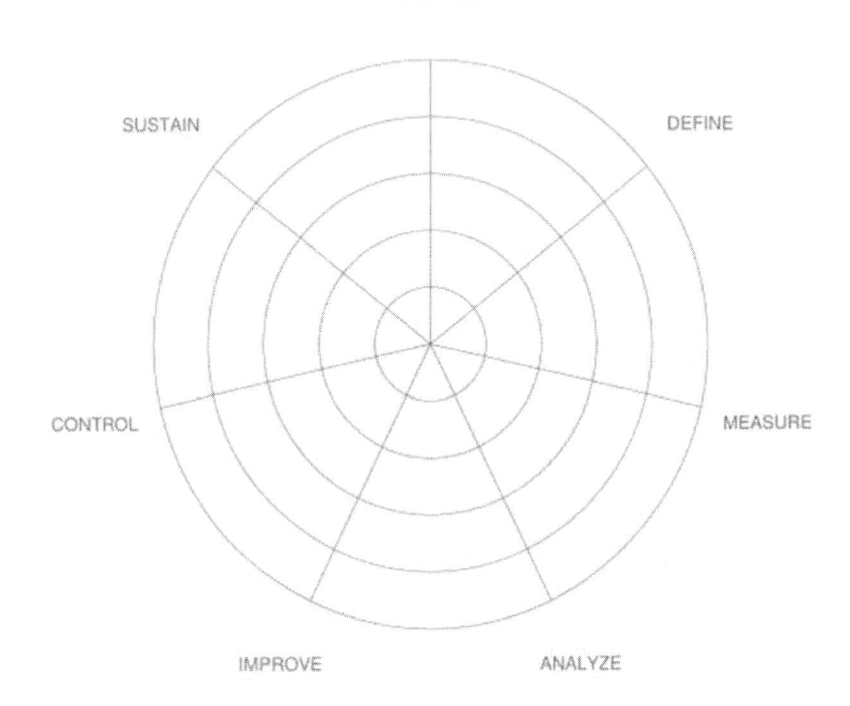

BEGINNING OF THE SELF-ASSESSMENT:

CRITERION #1: RECOGNIZE

INTENT: Be aware of the need for change. Recognize that there is an unfavorable variation, problem or symptom.

In my belief, the answer to this question is clearly defined:

5 Strongly Agree

4 Agree

3 Neutral

2 Disagree

1 Strongly Disagree

1. How do other organizations recognize emissions allowances?
<--- Score

2. How you do recognize revenue and expense and why?
<--- Score

3. How do you identify the kinds of information that

you will need?
<--- Score

4. What training and capacity building actions are needed to implement proposed reforms?
<--- Score

5. Do you need to report on all parts of your organization?
<--- Score

6. How far back in time do other organizations need to go?
<--- Score

7. Will new equipment/products be required to facilitate GHG Emissions Accounting delivery, for example is new software needed?
<--- Score

8. What extra resources will you need?
<--- Score

9. What are the GHG Emissions Accounting resources needed?
<--- Score

10. What GHG Emissions Accounting capabilities do you need?
<--- Score

11. Did you miss any major GHG Emissions Accounting issues?
<--- Score

12. Who else hopes to benefit from it?

<--- Score

13. How are purchased CERs initially recognized on the balance sheet?
<--- Score

14. As a sponsor, customer or management, how important is it to meet goals, objectives?
<--- Score

15. When do other organizations in scope need to report?
<--- Score

16. What information do users need?
<--- Score

17. What situation(s) led to this GHG Emissions Accounting Self Assessment?
<--- Score

18. Do you provide incentives for the management of climate change issues, including the attainment of targets?
<--- Score

19. Are there any specific expectations or concerns about the GHG Emissions Accounting team, GHG Emissions Accounting itself?
<--- Score

20. Where might there be quality problems, and how could be overcome?
<--- Score

21. Will a response program recognize when a crisis

occurs and provide some level of response?
<--- Score

22. What GHG Emissions Accounting problem should be solved?
<--- Score

23. What GHG Emissions Accounting coordination do you need?
<--- Score

24. How are the GHG Emissions Accounting's objectives aligned to the group's overall stakeholder strategy?
<--- Score

25. How do you assess your GHG Emissions Accounting workforce capability and capacity needs, including skills, competencies, and staffing levels?
<--- Score

26. What is the smallest subset of the problem you can usefully solve?
<--- Score

27. What are the stakeholder objectives to be achieved with GHG Emissions Accounting?
<--- Score

28. Are controls defined to recognize and contain problems?
<--- Score

29. Does GHG Emissions Accounting create potential expectations in other areas that need to be recognized and considered?

<--- Score

30. What are your needs in relation to GHG Emissions Accounting skills, labor, equipment, and markets?
<--- Score

31. Are employees recognized for desired behaviors?
<--- Score

32. Who needs to know?
<--- Score

33. Who should resolve the GHG Emissions Accounting issues?
<--- Score

34. To what extent does each concerned units management team recognize GHG Emissions Accounting as an effective investment?
<--- Score

35. Which needs are not included or involved?
<--- Score

36. Who defines the rules in relation to any given issue?
<--- Score

37. How do you recognize an GHG Emissions Accounting objection?
<--- Score

38. What would happen if GHG Emissions Accounting weren't done?
<--- Score

39. What other information do you need to move to a low emission transport sector?
<--- Score

40. How do you recognize an objection?
<--- Score

41. How do you identify subcontractor relationships?
<--- Score

42. Think about the people you identified for your GHG Emissions Accounting project and the project responsibilities you would assign to them, what kind of training do you think they would need to perform these responsibilities effectively?
<--- Score

43. What does GHG Emissions Accounting success mean to the stakeholders?
<--- Score

44. What are the expected benefits of GHG Emissions Accounting to the stakeholder?
<--- Score

45. How do you take a forward-looking perspective in identifying GHG Emissions Accounting research related to market response and models?
<--- Score

46. What prevents you from making the changes you know will make you a more effective GHG Emissions Accounting leader?
<--- Score

47. What tools and technologies are needed for a

custom GHG Emissions Accounting project?
<--- Score

48. What policy needs have the accounts helped address?
<--- Score

49. What needs to be done?
<--- Score

50. Are employees recognized or rewarded for performance that demonstrates the highest levels of integrity?
<--- Score

51. Are losses recognized in a timely manner?
<--- Score

52. What vendors make products that address the GHG Emissions Accounting needs?
<--- Score

53. How will carbon footprinting address the issues of mitigation, emissions trading, and/or marketing?
<--- Score

54. Where are granted allowances initially recognized on the balance sheet?
<--- Score

55. Why the need?
<--- Score

56. How are the liabilities for emissions recognized?

<--- Score

57. Have you identified your GHG Emissions Accounting key performance indicators?
<--- Score

58. How do you identify and calculate your organizations emission sources?
<--- Score

59. What activities does the governance board need to consider?
<--- Score

60. What problems are you facing and how do you consider GHG Emissions Accounting will circumvent those obstacles?
<--- Score

61. How do you identify your organizations emission sources?
<--- Score

62. Where is training needed?
<--- Score

63. How are training requirements identified?
<--- Score

64. For your GHG Emissions Accounting project, identify and describe the business environment, is there more than one layer to the business environment?
<--- Score

65. How much more energy infrastructure would

you need?
<--- Score

66. How many projects would have needed to be reviewed or abandoned?
<--- Score

67. How are purchased emissions allowances recognized?
<--- Score

68. Looking at each person individually – does every one have the qualities which are needed to work in this group?
<--- Score

69. What needs to stay?
<--- Score

70. When should purchased CERs be recognized?
<--- Score

71. How are you going to measure success?
<--- Score

72. What resources or support might you need?
<--- Score

73. How can the price which enables your organizations policies to be best supported and directed be identified?
<--- Score

74. What level of precision is needed at minimum to make judgments on differences over time?
<--- Score

75. How much are sponsors, customers, partners, stakeholders involved in GHG Emissions Accounting? In other words, what are the risks, if GHG Emissions Accounting does not deliver successfully?
<--- Score

Add up total points for this section:
_____ = Total points for this section

Divided by: ______ (number of statements answered) = ______
Average score for this section

Transfer your score to the GHG Emissions Accounting Index at the beginning of the Self-Assessment.

CRITERION #2: DEFINE:

INTENT: Formulate the stakeholder problem. Define the problem, needs and objectives.

In my belief, the answer to this question is clearly defined:

5 Strongly Agree

4 Agree

3 Neutral

2 Disagree

1 Strongly Disagree

1. When are meeting minutes sent out? Who is on the distribution list?
<--- Score

2. Is a fully trained team formed, supported, and committed to work on the GHG Emissions Accounting improvements?
<--- Score

3. Have the customer needs been translated into specific, measurable requirements? How?
<--- Score

4. What would be the goal or target for a GHG Emissions Accounting's improvement team?
<--- Score

5. Has anyone else (internal or external to the group) attempted to solve this problem or a similar one before? If so, what knowledge can be leveraged from these previous efforts?
<--- Score

6. What are the requirements for audit information?
<--- Score

7. When is/was the GHG Emissions Accounting start date?
<--- Score

8. What are the GHG Emissions Accounting tasks and definitions?
<--- Score

9. Is the team formed and are team leaders (Coaches and Management Leads) assigned?
<--- Score

10. Is there regularly 100% attendance at the team meetings? If not, have appointed substitutes attended to preserve cross-functionality and full representation?
<--- Score

11. Has the improvement team collected the 'voice of

the customer' (obtained feedback – qualitative and quantitative)?
<--- Score

12. Do you have a GHG Emissions Accounting success story or case study ready to tell and share?
<--- Score

13. Is GHG Emissions Accounting currently on schedule according to the plan?
<--- Score

14. Is the scope of GHG Emissions Accounting defined?
<--- Score

15. What is a worst-case scenario for losses?
<--- Score

16. Is the improvement team aware of the different versions of a process: what they think it is vs. what it actually is vs. what it should be vs. what it could be?
<--- Score

17. What sources do you use to gather information for a GHG Emissions Accounting study?
<--- Score

18. If substitutes have been appointed, have they been briefed on the GHG Emissions Accounting goals and received regular communications as to the progress to date?
<--- Score

19. Has/have the customer(s) been identified?
<--- Score

20. Has a team charter been developed and communicated?
<--- Score

21. What intelligence can you gather?
<--- Score

22. How do you hand over GHG Emissions Accounting context?
<--- Score

23. Are the GHG Emissions Accounting requirements complete?
<--- Score

24. What are the Roles and Responsibilities for each team member and its leadership? Where is this documented?
<--- Score

25. What are the legal, organizational, and technical frameworks for the required registry?
<--- Score

26. Is there a critical path to deliver GHG Emissions Accounting results?
<--- Score

27. Has the direction changed at all during the course of GHG Emissions Accounting? If so, when did it change and why?
<--- Score

28. What is the scope of the GHG Emissions Accounting work?

<--- Score

29. Is the work to date meeting requirements?
<--- Score

30. Is the GHG Emissions Accounting scope manageable?
<--- Score

31. How is the team tracking and documenting its work?
<--- Score

32. What are the rough order estimates on cost savings/opportunities that GHG Emissions Accounting brings?
<--- Score

33. What are the record-keeping requirements of GHG Emissions Accounting activities?
<--- Score

34. Who defines (or who defined) the rules and roles?
<--- Score

35. How will variation in the actual durations of each activity be dealt with to ensure that the expected GHG Emissions Accounting results are met?
<--- Score

36. Is the team sponsored by a champion or stakeholder leader?
<--- Score

37. How do you manage scope?
<--- Score

38. Are roles and responsibilities formally defined?
<--- Score

39. Is the current 'as is' process being followed? If not, what are the discrepancies?
<--- Score

40. Are team charters developed?
<--- Score

41. Is the team equipped with available and reliable resources?
<--- Score

42. Will team members regularly document their GHG Emissions Accounting work?
<--- Score

43. How will the GHG Emissions Accounting team and the group measure complete success of GHG Emissions Accounting?
<--- Score

44. How do you gather requirements?
<--- Score

45. How do you think the partners involved in GHG Emissions Accounting would have defined success?
<--- Score

46. What customer feedback methods were used to solicit their input?
<--- Score

47. Has a project plan, Gantt chart, or similar been

developed/completed?
<--- Score

48. What is the context?
<--- Score

49. Is GHG Emissions Accounting linked to key stakeholder goals and objectives?
<--- Score

50. In what way can you redefine the criteria of choice clients have in your category in your favor?
<--- Score

51. What are the boundaries of the scope? What is in bounds and what is not? What is the start point? What is the stop point?
<--- Score

52. Are stakeholder processes mapped?
<--- Score

53. Does the team have regular meetings?
<--- Score

54. Are customer(s) identified and segmented according to their different needs and requirements?
<--- Score

55. What key stakeholder process output measure(s) does GHG Emissions Accounting leverage and how?
<--- Score

56. Have all basic functions of GHG Emissions Accounting been defined?
<--- Score

57. Are customers identified and high impact areas defined?
<--- Score

58. Has the GHG Emissions Accounting work been fairly and/or equitably divided and delegated among team members who are qualified and capable to perform the work? Has everyone contributed?
<--- Score

59. Are there different segments of customers?
<--- Score

60. Has a high-level 'as is' process map been completed, verified and validated?
<--- Score

61. What knowledge or experience is required?
<--- Score

62. Who approved the GHG Emissions Accounting scope?
<--- Score

63. What is the scope of GHG Emissions Accounting?
<--- Score

64. How do you manage changes in GHG Emissions Accounting requirements?
<--- Score

65. Are there any constraints known that bear on the ability to perform GHG Emissions Accounting work? How is the team addressing them?
<--- Score

66. Is data collected and displayed to better understand customer(s) critical needs and requirements.
<--- Score

67. Do the reporting requirements link to implementation of targets?
<--- Score

68. Are different versions of process maps needed to account for the different types of inputs?
<--- Score

69. What are the dynamics of the communication plan?
<--- Score

70. How do you build the right business case?
<--- Score

71. Are your existing continuous disclosure reviews of corporate governance and environmental matters adequate to support compliance with the applicable disclosure requirements?
<--- Score

72. Are improvement team members fully trained on GHG Emissions Accounting?
<--- Score

73. How was the 'as is' process map developed, reviewed, verified and validated?
<--- Score

74. What scope to assess?
<--- Score

75. How are consistent GHG Emissions Accounting definitions important?
<--- Score

76. Do you have organizational privacy requirements?
<--- Score

77. Does the scope remain the same?
<--- Score

78. Do the problem and goal statements meet the SMART criteria (specific, measurable, attainable, relevant, and time-bound)?
<--- Score

79. How often are the team meetings?
<--- Score

80. What specifically is the problem? Where does it occur? When does it occur? What is its extent?
<--- Score

81. How can the value of GHG Emissions Accounting be defined?
<--- Score

82. Scope of sensitive information?
<--- Score

83. What are the compelling stakeholder reasons for embarking on GHG Emissions Accounting?
<--- Score

84. Is special GHG Emissions Accounting user knowledge required?
<--- Score

85. Who are the GHG Emissions Accounting improvement team members, including Management Leads and Coaches?
<--- Score

86. What is the definition of success?
<--- Score

87. What is in scope?
<--- Score

88. What constraints exist that might impact the team?
<--- Score

89. Has your scope been defined?
<--- Score

90. Is there a completed, verified, and validated high-level 'as is' (not 'should be' or 'could be') stakeholder process map?
<--- Score

91. Has everyone on the team, including the team leaders, been properly trained?
<--- Score

92. What is the scope of the GHG Emissions Accounting effort?
<--- Score

93. Will team members perform GHG Emissions

Accounting work when assigned and in a timely fashion?
<--- Score

94. How does the GHG Emissions Accounting manager ensure against scope creep?
<--- Score

95. Are task requirements clearly defined?
<--- Score

96. What defines best in class?
<--- Score

97. How do you catch GHG Emissions Accounting definition inconsistencies?
<--- Score

98. What is out-of-scope initially?
<--- Score

99. How did the GHG Emissions Accounting manager receive input to the development of a GHG Emissions Accounting improvement plan and the estimated completion dates/times of each activity?
<--- Score

100. Is there a GHG Emissions Accounting management charter, including stakeholder case, problem and goal statements, scope, milestones, roles and responsibilities, communication plan?
<--- Score

101. What resources are required for implementation?
<--- Score

102. Is full participation by members in regularly held team meetings guaranteed?
<--- Score

103. Is there any additional GHG Emissions Accounting definition of success?
<--- Score

104. Is the team adequately staffed with the desired cross-functionality? If not, what additional resources are available to the team?
<--- Score

105. When is the estimated completion date?
<--- Score

106. How would you define GHG Emissions Accounting leadership?
<--- Score

107. What critical content must be communicated – who, what, when, where, and how?
<--- Score

108. How do you keep key subject matter experts in the loop?
<--- Score

109. Will a GHG Emissions Accounting production readiness review be required?
<--- Score

110. Is there a completed SIPOC representation, describing the Suppliers, Inputs, Process, Outputs, and Customers?

<--- Score

111. What is the worst case scenario?
<--- Score

112. What scope do you want your strategy to cover?
<--- Score

113. Who is gathering GHG Emissions Accounting information?
<--- Score

Add up total points for this section:
_____ = Total points for this section

Divided by: ______ (number of statements answered) = ______ Average score for this section

Transfer your score to the GHG Emissions Accounting Index at the beginning of the Self-Assessment.

CRITERION #3: MEASURE:

INTENT: Gather the correct data.
Measure the current performance and
evolution of the situation.

In my belief, the answer to this
question is clearly defined:

5 Strongly Agree

4 Agree

3 Neutral

2 Disagree

1 Strongly Disagree

1. Does your organization systematically track and analyze outcomes related for accountability and quality improvement?
<--- Score

2. What impact does it have on land use?
<--- Score

3. Do you aggressively reward and promote the

people who have the biggest impact on creating excellent GHG Emissions Accounting services/ products?
<--- Score

4. What would be a real cause for concern?
<--- Score

5. Among the GHG Emissions Accounting product and service cost to be estimated, which is considered hardest to estimate?
<--- Score

6. What measurements are possible, practicable and meaningful?
<--- Score

7. Have any impacts from climate change, environmental degradation and/or natural hazards been felt?
<--- Score

8. What data was collected (past, present, future/ ongoing)?
<--- Score

9. How do your measurements capture actionable GHG Emissions Accounting information for use in exceeding your customers expectations and securing your customers engagement?
<--- Score

10. Why a GHG Emissions Accounting focus?
<--- Score

11. How will you measure success?

<--- Score

12. How can you measure the performance?
<--- Score

13. Which costs should be taken into account?
<--- Score

14. What particular quality tools did the team find helpful in establishing measurements?
<--- Score

15. How can a GHG Emissions Accounting test verify your ideas or assumptions?
<--- Score

16. How are carbon emissions measured and how are the boundaries set?
<--- Score

17. Have you found any 'ground fruit' or 'low-hanging fruit' for immediate remedies to the gap in performance?
<--- Score

18. Have any response to impacts been implemented?
<--- Score

19. How will the GHG Emissions Accounting data be analyzed?
<--- Score

20. How do you verify and develop ideas and innovations?
<--- Score

21. Have the types of risks that may impact GHG Emissions Accounting been identified and analyzed?
<--- Score

22. Are high impact defects defined and identified in the stakeholder process?
<--- Score

23. What are climate changes current and future impacts on organizations?
<--- Score

24. What is the cause of any GHG Emissions Accounting gaps?
<--- Score

25. Is there an opportunity to verify requirements?
<--- Score

26. What are your primary costs, revenues, assets?
<--- Score

27. What are the impacts of climate change?
<--- Score

28. What tools can be used to help assess the effectiveness of individual measures?
<--- Score

29. What are your customers expectations and measures?
<--- Score

30. How do the potential benefits of mitigation in terms of avoided impacts compare with mitigation

costs and with ancillary benefits?
<--- Score

31. What key measures identified indicate the performance of the stakeholder process?
<--- Score

32. What relevant entities could be measured?
<--- Score

33. How do you measure efficient delivery of GHG Emissions Accounting services?
<--- Score

34. Is there a Performance Baseline?
<--- Score

35. What is to be measured, reported and verified?
<--- Score

36. How do you measure success?
<--- Score

37. Does management have the right priorities among projects?
<--- Score

38. Which factors increase or reduce the capacity of people to reduce the impact of the activity?
<--- Score

39. Do you verify that corrective actions were taken?
<--- Score

40. What drives O&M cost?
<--- Score

41. Who participated in the data collection for measurements?
<--- Score

42. Are key measures identified and agreed upon?
<--- Score

43. Is data available on the types and quantities/ cost of fuels consumed during transportation?
<--- Score

44. Are indirect costs charged to the GHG Emissions Accounting program?
<--- Score

45. What are the current costs of the GHG Emissions Accounting process?
<--- Score

46. What are the costs of reform?
<--- Score

47. What is climate change and what are the impacts?
<--- Score

48. Does GHG Emissions Accounting systematically track and analyze outcomes for accountability and quality improvement?
<--- Score

49. What are the estimated costs of proposed changes?
<--- Score

50. What methods are feasible and acceptable to estimate the impact of reforms?
<--- Score

51. Are process variation components displayed/ communicated using suitable charts, graphs, plots?
<--- Score

52. Is key measure data collection planned and executed, process variation displayed and communicated and performance baselined?
<--- Score

53. How should consumption emissions be measured in a consistent and transparent way across countries?
<--- Score

54. Are the measures suited for enhancing the resilience of communities and system?
<--- Score

55. Do the benefits outweigh the costs?
<--- Score

56. Is Process Variation Displayed/Communicated?
<--- Score

57. What happens if cost savings do not materialize?
<--- Score

58. Is the solution cost-effective?
<--- Score

59. What is your GHG Emissions Accounting quality cost segregation study?

<--- Score

60. How can level of uncertainty be measured?
<--- Score

61. What are the GHG Emissions Accounting key cost drivers?
<--- Score

62. How will effects be measured?
<--- Score

63. What users will be impacted?
<--- Score

64. Are there any easy-to-implement alternatives to GHG Emissions Accounting? Sometimes other solutions are available that do not require the cost implications of a full-blown project?
<--- Score

65. How do you measure variability?
<--- Score

66. How is the value delivered by GHG Emissions Accounting being measured?
<--- Score

67. Why do the measurements/indicators matter?
<--- Score

68. How to cause the change?
<--- Score

69. What are the agreed upon definitions of the high impact areas, defect(s), unit(s), and opportunities that

will figure into the process capability metrics?
<--- Score

70. What is measured? Why?
<--- Score

71. Is there a significant risk that substantial negative impacts are caused by the activity?
<--- Score

72. What causes investor action?
<--- Score

73. Has your organization considered the impact of climate change on its investment portfolio?
<--- Score

74. How do you verify the GHG Emissions Accounting requirements quality?
<--- Score

75. What are the uncertainties surrounding estimates of impact?
<--- Score

76. Is long term and short term variability accounted for?
<--- Score

77. How do you focus on what is right -not who is right?
<--- Score

78. What has the team done to assure the stability and accuracy of the measurement process?
<--- Score

79. Who is involved in verifying compliance?
<--- Score

80. What is the GHG Emissions Accounting business impact?
<--- Score

81. How do you aggregate measures across priorities?
<--- Score

82. When a disaster occurs, who gets priority?
<--- Score

83. Has a cost center been established?
<--- Score

84. How do you verify if GHG Emissions Accounting is built right?
<--- Score

85. Is a solid data collection plan established that includes measurement systems analysis?
<--- Score

86. Is data collection planned and executed?
<--- Score

87. What could cause you to change course?
<--- Score

88. Where is it measured?
<--- Score

89. Can you do GHG Emissions Accounting without complex (expensive) analysis?

<--- Score

90. How will costs be allocated?
<--- Score

91. What are allowable costs?
<--- Score

92. How will your organization measure success?
<--- Score

93. Was a data collection plan established?
<--- Score

94. Is data collected on key measures that were identified?
<--- Score

95. Are actual costs in line with budgeted costs?
<--- Score

96. How is progress measured?
<--- Score

97. How do you stay flexible and focused to recognize larger GHG Emissions Accounting results?
<--- Score

98. What do people want to verify?
<--- Score

99. How sensitive must the GHG Emissions Accounting strategy be to cost?
<--- Score

100. How will success or failure be measured?

<--- Score

101. Are the measurements objective?
<--- Score

102. What are the key input variables? What are the key process variables? What are the key output variables?
<--- Score

103. Does GHG Emissions Accounting analysis isolate the fundamental causes of problems?
<--- Score

104. Where is the cost?
<--- Score

105. How do you do risk analysis of rare, cascading, catastrophic events?
<--- Score

106. Can management and accounting practices decrease your organizations environmental impacts?
<--- Score

107. Have any impacts from climate change and/or disaster risk been felt?
<--- Score

108. The approach of traditional GHG Emissions Accounting works for detail complexity but is focused on a systematic approach rather than an understanding of the nature of systems themselves, what approach will permit your organization to deal with the kind of unpredictable emergent behaviors

that dynamic complexity can introduce?
<--- Score

109. How do you control the overall costs of your work processes?
<--- Score

110. Do you effectively measure and reward individual and team performance?
<--- Score

111. How will you measure your GHG Emissions Accounting effectiveness?
<--- Score

112. How long to keep data and how to manage retention costs?
<--- Score

113. What charts has the team used to display the components of variation in the process?
<--- Score

114. How large is the gap between current performance and the customer-specified (goal) performance?
<--- Score

115. What details are required of the GHG Emissions Accounting cost structure?
<--- Score

116. Can you measure the return on analysis?
<--- Score

117. Will new emissions trading regulations add

new costs to the business?
<--- Score

118. Who should receive measurement reports?
<--- Score

119. Is the activity in a sector which potentially causes greenhouse gas emissions?
<--- Score

120. What are the envisaged effects of climate mitigation and adaptation policies on autonomous developments and on the impact of existing policies?
<--- Score

121. Is it to be able to establish policies, what is impacting it?
<--- Score

122. When is Root Cause Analysis Required?
<--- Score

123. What are you verifying?
<--- Score

124. Where can you go to verify the info?
<--- Score

125. What can be used to verify compliance?
<--- Score

126. How is performance measured?
<--- Score

127. Is the cost worth the GHG Emissions Accounting

effort ?
<--- Score

128. What are your key GHG Emissions Accounting indicators that you will measure, analyze and track?
<--- Score

Add up total points for this section:
_____ = Total points for this section

Divided by: ______ (number of statements answered) = ______ Average score for this section

Transfer your score to the GHG Emissions Accounting Index at the beginning of the Self-Assessment.

CRITERION #4: ANALYZE:

INTENT: Analyze causes, assumptions and hypotheses.

In my belief, the answer to this question is clearly defined:

5 Strongly Agree

4 Agree

3 Neutral

2 Disagree

1 Strongly Disagree

1. What qualifications are needed?
<--- Score

2. What kind of crime could a potential new hire have committed that would not only not disqualify him/her from being hired by your organization, but would actually indicate that he/she might be a particularly good fit?
<--- Score

3. What are your current levels and trends in key measures or indicators of GHG Emissions Accounting product and process performance that are important to and directly serve your customers? How do these results compare with the performance of your competitors and other organizations with similar offerings?
<--- Score

4. What is the complexity of the output produced?
<--- Score

5. How long has the dataset existed and how extensively has it been used?
<--- Score

6. What tools were used to generate the list of possible causes?
<--- Score

7. What are the revised rough estimates of the financial savings/opportunity for GHG Emissions Accounting improvements?
<--- Score

8. Is it conditions at the time data were collected?
<--- Score

9. What is the output?
<--- Score

10. Are data available for intermittent years only?
<--- Score

11. What reporting processes are needed?
<--- Score

12. How is data used for program management and improvement?
<--- Score

13. Is the required GHG Emissions Accounting data gathered?
<--- Score

14. How will the GHG Emissions Accounting data be captured?
<--- Score

15. Was a cause-and-effect diagram used to explore the different types of causes (or sources of variation)?
<--- Score

16. What period should you collect data for?
<--- Score

17. Is data already being collected?
<--- Score

18. How does climate change present general opportunities for your organization?
<--- Score

19. What GHG Emissions Accounting metrics are outputs of the process?
<--- Score

20. How to establish an efficient data collection system?
<--- Score

21. How was the detailed process map generated,

verified, and validated?
<--- Score

22. How difficult is it to qualify what GHG Emissions Accounting ROI is?
<--- Score

23. What is your organizations process which leads to recognition of value generation?
<--- Score

24. What conclusions were drawn from the team's data collection and analysis? How did the team reach these conclusions?
<--- Score

25. Are gaps between current performance and the goal performance identified?
<--- Score

26. Was a detailed process map created to amplify critical steps of the 'as is' stakeholder process?
<--- Score

27. Do the policy instruments work best in isolation or are there significant opportunities for instruments to complement one another?
<--- Score

28. How do you move quickly from carbon accounting listed equity to corporate credits?
<--- Score

29. Can the capture process be changed to obtain the data?
<--- Score

30. How to deal with the non linear relationship between research inputs and outputs?
<--- Score

31. Think about some of the processes you undertake within your organization, which do you own?
<--- Score

32. Is the data original or estimated from other data sources?
<--- Score

33. How do you promote understanding that opportunity for improvement is not criticism of the status quo, or the people who created the status quo?
<--- Score

34. How has the GHG Emissions Accounting data been gathered?
<--- Score

35. Where in the value chain does the opportunity occur?
<--- Score

36. Why is there a distinction for historical data?
<--- Score

37. Is data and process analysis, root cause analysis and quantifying the gap/opportunity in place?
<--- Score

38. What qualifies as competition?
<--- Score

39. How does the organization define, manage, and improve its GHG Emissions Accounting processes?
<--- Score

40. Are you missing GHG Emissions Accounting opportunities?
<--- Score

41. What are the personnel training and qualifications required?
<--- Score

42. What GHG Emissions Accounting data should be collected?
<--- Score

43. What were the crucial 'moments of truth' on the process map?
<--- Score

44. Do physical changes resulting from climate change present opportunities for your organization?
<--- Score

45. Who owns what data?
<--- Score

46. Does climate change present other opportunities for your organization?
<--- Score

47. What methods do you use to drive investment in emissions reduction activities?
<--- Score

48. How are outputs preserved and protected?
<--- Score

49. Do regulatory requirements on climate change present opportunities for your organization?
<--- Score

50. What is the cost of poor quality as supported by the team's analysis?
<--- Score

51. What output to create?
<--- Score

52. Do quality systems drive continuous improvement?
<--- Score

53. How should carbon pricing be integrated into accounting processes?
<--- Score

54. Do you use existing emissions data?
<--- Score

55. Is there any risk that the data will be perceived as biased?
<--- Score

56. What tools were used to narrow the list of possible causes?
<--- Score

57. How is GHG Emissions Accounting data gathered?
<--- Score

58. How can risk management be tied procedurally to process elements?
<--- Score

59. What data collection activities and data management issues do your operational facilities have to deal with?
<--- Score

60. Who is involved in the process of data collection and review?
<--- Score

61. What are the best opportunities for value improvement?
<--- Score

62. What are evaluation criteria for the output?
<--- Score

63. Are thorough descriptions of data collection, management, and review processes included?
<--- Score

64. Have the accounts been used in policy processes related to climate change mitigation or adaptation?
<--- Score

65. What are your key performance measures or indicators and in-process measures for the control and improvement of your GHG Emissions Accounting processes?
<--- Score

66. Should you invest in industry-recognized

qualifications?
<--- Score

67. Did any value-added analysis or 'lean thinking' take place to identify some of the gaps shown on the 'as is' process map?
<--- Score

68. Is the suppliers process defined and controlled?
<--- Score

69. Have you identified any inherent climate change opportunities that have the potential to generate a substantive change in your business operations, revenue or expenditure?
<--- Score

70. Do you, as a leader, bounce back quickly from setbacks?
<--- Score

71. Have any additional benefits been identified that will result from closing all or most of the gaps?
<--- Score

72. What systems/processes must you excel at?
<--- Score

73. Do you have data about solutions?
<--- Score

74. Who will gather what data?
<--- Score

75. What does the data say about the performance of the stakeholder process?

<--- Score

76. How do you identify specific GHG Emissions Accounting investment opportunities and emerging trends?
<--- Score

77. Were any designed experiments used to generate additional insight into the data analysis?
<--- Score

78. Does climate change present any economic opportunities for your organization?
<--- Score

79. What other organizational variables, such as reward systems or communication systems, affect the performance of this GHG Emissions Accounting process?
<--- Score

80. Where is the data coming from to measure compliance?
<--- Score

81. Can you add value to the current GHG Emissions Accounting decision-making process (largely qualitative) by incorporating uncertainty modeling (more quantitative)?
<--- Score

82. What are the main sources of uncertainty in your data gathering, handling and calculations?
<--- Score

83. Is there any way to speed up the process?

<--- Score

84. How does your contractual purchasing drive change in low-carbon energy supply over time?
<--- Score

85. What emissions data do you need to report?
<--- Score

86. Is data assessed to be sufficiently representative?
<--- Score

87. Did any additional data need to be collected?
<--- Score

88. How many days a week do you drive alone to work?
<--- Score

89. Do you understand your management processes today?
<--- Score

90. What were the financial benefits resulting from any 'ground fruit or low-hanging fruit' (quick fixes)?
<--- Score

91. An organizationally feasible system request is one that considers the mission, goals and objectives of the organization, key questions are: is the GHG Emissions Accounting solution request practical and will it solve a problem or take advantage of an opportunity to achieve company goals?
<--- Score

92. What is the stakeholder process?
<--- Score

93. How frequently is the dataset updated?
<--- Score

94. Who will facilitate the team and process?
<--- Score

95. What is the basis of participation and what will happen to the data received?
<--- Score

96. Do your contracts/agreements contain data security obligations?
<--- Score

97. What information qualified as important?
<--- Score

98. How do you use GHG Emissions Accounting data and information to support organizational decision making and innovation?
<--- Score

99. How to address uncertainty on data sets?
<--- Score

100. What training and qualifications will you need?
<--- Score

101. Have the problem and goal statements been updated to reflect the additional knowledge gained from the analyze phase?
<--- Score

102. Is the gap/opportunity displayed and communicated in financial terms?
<--- Score

103. How will corresponding data be collected?
<--- Score

104. Should you get your emissions data verified?
<--- Score

105. How will the data be checked for quality?
<--- Score

106. How will data be used to determine emissions?
<--- Score

107. What quality tools were used to get through the analyze phase?
<--- Score

108. What are the GHG Emissions Accounting design outputs?
<--- Score

109. What are the processes for audit reporting and management?
<--- Score

110. When should a process be art not science?
<--- Score

111. Are data available on the physical quantity of the purchased good or service?
<--- Score

112. What process improvements will be needed?
<--- Score

113. Is the performance gap determined?
<--- Score

114. Were there any improvement opportunities identified from the process analysis?
<--- Score

115. What is the main data challenge in producing an air emissions account?
<--- Score

116. What internal processes need improvement?
<--- Score

117. A compounding model resolution with available relevant data can often provide insight towards a solution methodology; which GHG Emissions Accounting models, tools and techniques are necessary?
<--- Score

118. Is the GHG Emissions Accounting process severely broken such that a re-design is necessary?
<--- Score

119. How do you move quickly from footprinting listed equity to corporate credits?
<--- Score

120. What type of vehicle do you usually drive?
<--- Score

121. Do you see significant opportunities of

reducing greenhouse emissions by the activity?
<--- Score

122. What process should you select for improvement?
<--- Score

123. What are the risks and opportunities for your organization in terms of climate and energy?
<--- Score

124. What qualifications and skills do you need?
<--- Score

125. What GHG Emissions Accounting data should be managed?
<--- Score

126. How do your work systems and key work processes relate to and capitalize on your core competencies?
<--- Score

127. Which parts of your organization do you need to collect data from?
<--- Score

128. What resources go in to get the desired output?
<--- Score

129. What did the team gain from developing a sub-process map?
<--- Score

130. What GHG Emissions Accounting data will be collected?

<--- Score

131. How will the change process be managed?
<--- Score

132. Is there a strict change management process?
<--- Score

133. Were Pareto charts (or similar) used to portray the 'heavy hitters' (or key sources of variation)?
<--- Score

134. What, related to, GHG Emissions Accounting processes does your organization outsource?
<--- Score

135. Are distance activity data by vehicle type available?
<--- Score

Add up total points for this section:
_____ = Total points for this section

Divided by: ______ (number of statements answered) = ______ Average score for this section

Transfer your score to the GHG Emissions Accounting Index at the beginning of the Self-Assessment.

CRITERION #5: IMPROVE:

INTENT: Develop a practical solution. Innovate, establish and test the solution and to measure the results.

In my belief, the answer to this question is clearly defined:

5 Strongly Agree

4 Agree

3 Neutral

2 Disagree

1 Strongly Disagree

1. Have the accounts influenced decisions made or the adoption of policies relating to climate change adaptation or mitigation?
<--- Score

2. Risk events: what are the things that could go wrong?
<--- Score

3. Who are the GHG Emissions Accounting decision makers?
<--- Score

4. What attendant changes will need to be made to ensure that the solution is successful?
<--- Score

5. Explorations of the frontiers of GHG Emissions Accounting will help you build influence, improve GHG Emissions Accounting, optimize decision making, and sustain change, what is your approach?
<--- Score

6. Is supporting GHG Emissions Accounting documentation required?
<--- Score

7. How can you improve GHG Emissions Accounting?
<--- Score

8. Are procedures documented for managing GHG Emissions Accounting risks?
<--- Score

9. Risk factors: what are the characteristics of GHG Emissions Accounting that make it risky?
<--- Score

10. Are the key business and technology risks being managed?
<--- Score

11. How do you keep improving GHG Emissions Accounting?
<--- Score

12. What is the GHG Emissions Accounting's sustainability risk?
<--- Score

13. How is your organization exposed to regulatory risks related to climate change?
<--- Score

14. Are risk management tasks balanced centrally and locally?
<--- Score

15. How do you understand uncertainty in emission inventories?
<--- Score

16. To what extent does management recognize GHG Emissions Accounting as a tool to increase the results?
<--- Score

17. Is your organization exposed to other risks as a result of climate change?
<--- Score

18. What is the risk?
<--- Score

19. What tools were used to evaluate the potential solutions?
<--- Score

20. Where do you need GHG Emissions Accounting improvement?
<--- Score

21. Has the overall resilience of affected systems been improved?
<--- Score

22. How does your organization evaluate strategic GHG Emissions Accounting success?
<--- Score

23. What is GHG Emissions Accounting risk?
<--- Score

24. Do you have the optimal project management team structure?
<--- Score

25. Does climate change present other significant risks current and/or anticipated for your organization?
<--- Score

26. Is there a high likelihood that any recommendations will achieve their intended results?
<--- Score

27. What is the implementation plan?
<--- Score

28. Who are the GHG Emissions Accounting decision-makers?
<--- Score

29. Do environmental management systems improve business performance in an international setting?
<--- Score

30. What communications are necessary to support the implementation of the solution?
<--- Score

31. Should disclosure include information in areas found in the reporting regimes of other jurisdictions, as risk management and shareholder engagement?
<--- Score

32. What is the team's contingency plan for potential problems occurring in implementation?
<--- Score

33. What improves environmental compliance?
<--- Score

34. Who are the people involved in developing and implementing GHG Emissions Accounting?
<--- Score

35. What are the affordable GHG Emissions Accounting risks?
<--- Score

36. How do you improve productivity?
<--- Score

37. How is knowledge sharing about risk management improved?
<--- Score

38. Are you assessing GHG Emissions Accounting and risk?
<--- Score

39. Who should make the GHG Emissions Accounting decisions?
<--- Score

40. Are there significant risks for the strategy?
<--- Score

41. Where do the GHG Emissions Accounting decisions reside?
<--- Score

42. What error proofing will be done to address some of the discrepancies observed in the 'as is' process?
<--- Score

43. How will you know that you have improved?
<--- Score

44. Which GHG Emissions Accounting solution is appropriate?
<--- Score

45. Who makes the GHG Emissions Accounting decisions in your organization?
<--- Score

46. What resources are required for the improvement efforts?
<--- Score

47. How did / will your organization decide which option was the most appropriate?
<--- Score

48. What is the strategy for responding to physical risks arising from climate change?

<--- Score

49. What improvements have been achieved?
<--- Score

50. How far into the future are risks considered?
<--- Score

51. What are the concrete GHG Emissions Accounting results?
<--- Score

52. What went well, what should change, what can improve?
<--- Score

53. How do you define the solutions' scope?
<--- Score

54. Who manages supplier risk management in your organization?
<--- Score

55. Why improve in the first place?
<--- Score

56. How does the team improve its work?
<--- Score

57. How significant is the improvement in the eyes of the end user?
<--- Score

58. What tools were most useful during the improve phase?
<--- Score

59. How do you decide how much to remunerate an employee?
<--- Score

60. Have you identified breakpoints and/or risk tolerances that will trigger broad consideration of a potential need for intervention or modification of strategy?
<--- Score

61. How risky is your organization?
<--- Score

62. Have disaster risks been adequately considered in the strategy?
<--- Score

63. What tools were used to tap into the creativity and encourage 'outside the box' thinking?
<--- Score

64. Was a GHG Emissions Accounting charter developed?
<--- Score

65. How is your organization exposed to general risks as a result of climate change?
<--- Score

66. How do you mitigate GHG Emissions Accounting risk?
<--- Score

67. What were the underlying assumptions on the cost-benefit analysis?

<--- Score

68. Is the solution technically practical?
<--- Score

69. Is GHG Emissions Accounting documentation maintained?
<--- Score

70. What risks and advantages are associated to the different policy scenarios?
<--- Score

71. Can you integrate quality management and risk management?
<--- Score

72. Who manages GHG Emissions Accounting risk?
<--- Score

73. Does your organization evaluate its supply chain in relation to the environmental performance of its suppliers and subcontractors?
<--- Score

74. Who do you report GHG Emissions Accounting results to?
<--- Score

75. Do the viable solutions scale to future needs?
<--- Score

76. How is adaptation different from regular development?
<--- Score

77. GHG Emissions Accounting risk decisions: whose call Is It?
<--- Score

78. Can you identify any significant risks or exposures to GHG Emissions Accounting third- parties (vendors, service providers, alliance partners etc) that concern you?
<--- Score

79. What current systems have to be understood and/ or changed?
<--- Score

80. Are the risks fully understood, reasonable and manageable?
<--- Score

81. Do current and/or anticipated effects of climate change present significant physical risks to your organization?
<--- Score

82. How do you measure risk?
<--- Score

83. What assumptions are made about the solution and approach?
<--- Score

84. At what point will vulnerability assessments be performed once GHG Emissions Accounting is put into production (e.g., ongoing Risk Management after implementation)?
<--- Score

85. How should decision makers approach the issue of climate change?
<--- Score

86. How can skill-level changes improve GHG Emissions Accounting?
<--- Score

87. How can the phases of GHG Emissions Accounting development be identified?
<--- Score

88. How do you improve GHG Emissions Accounting service perception, and satisfaction?
<--- Score

89. How do you measure progress and evaluate training effectiveness?
<--- Score

90. Does the goal represent a desired result that can be measured?
<--- Score

91. What information on corporate governance and environmental matters would a reasonable investor need in order to make investment decisions?
<--- Score

92. What tools do you use once you have decided on a GHG Emissions Accounting strategy and more importantly how do you choose?
<--- Score

93. How will you measure the results?

<--- Score

94. How do you manage and improve your GHG Emissions Accounting work systems to deliver customer value and achieve organizational success and sustainability?
<--- Score

95. Is your organization exposed to physical risks from climate change?
<--- Score

96. Have natural disaster risks been adequately considered in the strategy?
<--- Score

97. Are risk triggers captured?
<--- Score

98. Do the solutions for emerging economies differ from developed economies?
<--- Score

99. How do the GHG Emissions Accounting results compare with the performance of your competitors and other organizations with similar offerings?
<--- Score

100. Who will be using the results of the measurement activities?
<--- Score

101. Which of the recognised risks out of all risks can be most likely transferred?
<--- Score

102. Are the most efficient solutions problem-specific?
<--- Score

103. Do you need to do a usability evaluation?
<--- Score

104. How is your organization exposed to physical risks from climate change?
<--- Score

105. For estimation problems, how do you develop an estimation statement?
<--- Score

106. Who controls key decisions that will be made?
<--- Score

107. What actually has to improve and by how much?
<--- Score

108. Are the emission results for use in evaluating project level emission results?
<--- Score

109. What lessons, if any, from a pilot were incorporated into the design of the full-scale solution?
<--- Score

110. What alternative responses are available to manage risk?
<--- Score

111. How do you manage GHG Emissions Accounting risk?
<--- Score

112. Will the controls trigger any other risks?
<--- Score

113. Do you know all specific solutions?
<--- Score

114. What are adaptation and risk reduction options?
<--- Score

115. Is there any other GHG Emissions Accounting solution?
<--- Score

116. What emissions are a result of your business, and belong to another entity?
<--- Score

117. How do you link measurement and risk?
<--- Score

118. How is continuous improvement applied to risk management?
<--- Score

119. Do those selected for the GHG Emissions Accounting team have a good general understanding of what GHG Emissions Accounting is all about?
<--- Score

120. For decision problems, how do you develop a decision statement?
<--- Score

121. What does the 'should be' process map/design look like?

<--- Score

122. Do you combine technical expertise with business knowledge and GHG Emissions Accounting Key topics include lifecycles, development approaches, requirements and how to make a business case?
<--- Score

123. Can the solution be designed and implemented within an acceptable time period?
<--- Score

124. Is the GHG Emissions Accounting solution sustainable?
<--- Score

125. What is the magnitude of the improvements?
<--- Score

126. What risks does climate change present for the energy industry?
<--- Score

127. What is GHG Emissions Accounting's impact on utilizing the best solution(s)?
<--- Score

128. What strategies for GHG Emissions Accounting improvement are successful?
<--- Score

129. What are the GHG Emissions Accounting security risks?
<--- Score

Add up total points for this section:
_____ = Total points for this section

Divided by: ______ (number of statements answered) = ______ Average score for this section

Transfer your score to the GHG Emissions Accounting Index at the beginning of the Self-Assessment.

CRITERION #6: CONTROL:

INTENT: Implement the practical solution. Maintain the performance and correct possible complications.

In my belief, the answer to this question is clearly defined:

5 Strongly Agree

4 Agree

3 Neutral

2 Disagree

1 Strongly Disagree

1. Do you have a plan for increasing your organizations resilience to the expected physical effects of climate change?
<--- Score

2. What other systems, operations, processes, and infrastructures (hiring practices, staffing, training, incentives/rewards, metrics/dashboards/scorecards, etc.) need updates, additions, changes, or deletions

in order to facilitate knowledge transfer and improvements?
<--- Score

3. What quality tools were useful in the control phase?
<--- Score

4. How widespread is its use?
<--- Score

5. What should the next improvement project be that is related to GHG Emissions Accounting?
<--- Score

6. What are customers monitoring?
<--- Score

7. Who is the GHG Emissions Accounting process owner?
<--- Score

8. Are new process steps, standards, and documentation ingrained into normal operations?
<--- Score

9. Is there a recommended audit plan for routine surveillance inspections of GHG Emissions Accounting's gains?
<--- Score

10. Are the GHG Emissions Accounting standards challenging?
<--- Score

11. How do you monitor usage and cost?
<--- Score

12. Has the strategy to be adjusted due to the identified climate and disaster risks?
<--- Score

13. What is the recommended frequency of auditing?
<--- Score

14. Is there a standardized process?
<--- Score

15. Is there a control plan in place for sustaining improvements (short and long-term)?
<--- Score

16. In the case of a GHG Emissions Accounting project, the criteria for the audit derive from implementation objectives, an audit of a GHG Emissions Accounting project involves assessing whether the recommendations outlined for implementation have been met, can you track that any GHG Emissions Accounting project is implemented as planned, and is it working?
<--- Score

17. Can support from partners be adjusted?
<--- Score

18. Which subpart takes precedence in your monitoring methodology?
<--- Score

19. Will your goals reflect your program budget?
<--- Score

20. Are the planned controls in place?

<--- Score

21. Who has control over resources?
<--- Score

22. What are the critical parameters to watch?
<--- Score

23. What key inputs and outputs are being measured on an ongoing basis?
<--- Score

24. What do your reports reflect?
<--- Score

25. Does a troubleshooting guide exist or is it needed?
<--- Score

26. Are there documented procedures?
<--- Score

27. How will input, process, and output variables be checked to detect for sub-optimal conditions?
<--- Score

28. Who will be in control?
<--- Score

29. What is the control/monitoring plan?
<--- Score

30. How is change control managed?
<--- Score

31. Is there an action plan in case of emergencies?
<--- Score

32. Will existing staff require re-training, for example, to learn new business processes?
<--- Score

33. Is there a documented and implemented monitoring plan?
<--- Score

34. How will the process owner verify improvement in present and future sigma levels, process capabilities?
<--- Score

35. How will new or emerging customer needs/requirements be checked/communicated to orient the process toward meeting the new specifications and continually reducing variation?
<--- Score

36. Who is going to spread your message?
<--- Score

37. How will the day-to-day responsibilities for monitoring and continual improvement be transferred from the improvement team to the process owner?
<--- Score

38. Who sets the GHG Emissions Accounting standards?
<--- Score

39. What other areas of the group might benefit from the GHG Emissions Accounting team's improvements, knowledge, and learning?
<--- Score

40. Is the GHG Emissions Accounting test/monitoring cost justified?
<--- Score

41. Does the response plan contain a definite closed loop continual improvement scheme (e.g., plan-do-check-act)?
<--- Score

42. Are operating procedures consistent?
<--- Score

43. How will report readings be checked to effectively monitor performance?
<--- Score

44. What will be the overall impact of the institutions plan on societal emissions?
<--- Score

45. Are the planned controls working?
<--- Score

46. What GHG Emissions Accounting standards are applicable?
<--- Score

47. How might the group capture best practices and lessons learned so as to leverage improvements?
<--- Score

48. Have new or revised work instructions resulted?
<--- Score

49. Is there documentation that will support the

successful operation of the improvement?
<--- Score

50. Is new knowledge gained imbedded in the response plan?
<--- Score

51. What are the issues that are informing the consideration on the standards?
<--- Score

52. How do your controls stack up?
<--- Score

53. Is there a GHG Emissions Accounting Communication plan covering who needs to get what information when?
<--- Score

54. Will any special training be provided for results interpretation?
<--- Score

55. How do you select, collect, align, and integrate GHG Emissions Accounting data and information for tracking daily operations and overall organizational performance, including progress relative to strategic objectives and action plans?
<--- Score

56. Is knowledge gained on process shared and institutionalized?
<--- Score

57. What adjustments to the strategies are needed?
<--- Score

58. What is the standard for acceptable GHG Emissions Accounting performance?
<--- Score

59. How will the process owner and team be able to hold the gains?
<--- Score

60. Do you monitor the effectiveness of your GHG Emissions Accounting activities?
<--- Score

61. What should you measure to verify efficiency gains?
<--- Score

62. Does the GHG Emissions Accounting performance meet the customer's requirements?
<--- Score

63. Does the strategy need to be adjusted due to the identified disaster risks?
<--- Score

64. Against what alternative is success being measured?
<--- Score

65. Is a response plan in place for when the input, process, or output measures indicate an 'out-of-control' condition?
<--- Score

66. What are the key elements of your GHG Emissions Accounting performance improvement system,

including your evaluation, organizational learning, and innovation processes?
<--- Score

67. What is your plan to assess your security risks?
<--- Score

68. Does job training on the documented procedures need to be part of the process team's education and training?
<--- Score

69. How should the climate regime adjust to ensure efficient and equitable outcomes?
<--- Score

70. Is reporting being used or needed?
<--- Score

71. Are suggested corrective/restorative actions indicated on the response plan for known causes to problems that might surface?
<--- Score

72. Is there a transfer of ownership and knowledge to process owner and process team tasked with the responsibilities.
<--- Score

73. Are documented procedures clear and easy to follow for the operators?
<--- Score

74. Is a response plan established and deployed?
<--- Score

75. Where do you find guidance on quality control and assessing uncertainty?
<--- Score

76. Has the improved process and its steps been standardized?
<--- Score

Add up total points for this section:
_____ = Total points for this section

Divided by: ______ (number of statements answered) = ______ Average score for this section

Transfer your score to the GHG Emissions Accounting Index at the beginning of the Self-Assessment.

CRITERION #7: SUSTAIN:

INTENT: Retain the benefits.

In my belief, the answer to this question is clearly defined:

5 Strongly Agree

4 Agree

3 Neutral

2 Disagree

1 Strongly Disagree

1. What are the barriers to increased GHG Emissions Accounting production?
<--- Score

2. What is the correct level for your organizations internal prices?
<--- Score

3. What GHG Emissions Accounting modifications can you make work for you?
<--- Score

4. How do you value your carbon credits and carbon sinks?
<--- Score

5. What is your BATNA (best alternative to a negotiated agreement)?
<--- Score

6. Do you think you know, or do you know you know ?
<--- Score

7. What must you excel at?
<--- Score

8. Where is the highest level of direct responsibility for climate change within your organization?
<--- Score

9. What, however, could be causing the land to take up more carbon than it releases each year?
<--- Score

10. What are the relevant factors influencing current and future vulnerability?
<--- Score

11. Where is the highest level of responsibility for climate change within your organization?
<--- Score

12. What kind of utilities have the highest targeted levels of carbon reduction?
<--- Score

13. What are the rules for biofuel carbon accounting?
<--- Score

14. Can your business participate in any projects, offsets or credit mechanisms?
<--- Score

15. Which organization facilities and emission sources should be included?
<--- Score

16. Is the option targeting the most vulnerable communities/people?
<--- Score

17. What would have to be true for the option on the table to be the best possible choice?
<--- Score

18. Is there a preliminary geo reference to the projects/programs intended location?
<--- Score

19. If there were zero limitations, what would you do differently?
<--- Score

20. How should practitioners value carbon credits and carbon sinks?
<--- Score

21. When does organizational investor activism pay?
<--- Score

22. What makes good climate change governance?
<--- Score

23. Do emissions for the reporting year vary significantly compared to previous years?
<--- Score

24. What is the kind of project structure that would be appropriate for your GHG Emissions Accounting project, should it be formal and complex, or can it be less formal and relatively simple?
<--- Score

25. Do you participate in any emission trading schemes?
<--- Score

26. How do you ensure consistency in uncertainty assessment among different sectors?
<--- Score

27. What kind of person makes an ideal climate champion?
<--- Score

28. What are some main sources of change in the capacity to sequester carbon?
<--- Score

29. Will your organization include emissions from transportation?
<--- Score

30. What are the top 3 things at the forefront of your GHG Emissions Accounting agendas for the next 3 years?

<--- Score

31. What should be the role for new technologies in slowing climate change?
<--- Score

32. In retrospect, of the projects that you pulled the plug on, what percent do you wish had been allowed to keep going, and what percent do you wish had ended earlier?
<--- Score

33. What emission reduction tools are already in place?
<--- Score

34. Are you maintaining a past–present–future perspective throughout the GHG Emissions Accounting discussion?
<--- Score

35. Can the selected indicators be attributed directly or indirectly to the effects of climate change?
<--- Score

36. Are you making progress, and are you making progress as GHG Emissions Accounting leaders?
<--- Score

37. What is the make and model of your vehicle?
<--- Score

38. What will your future climate be like?
<--- Score

39. How do you listen to customers to obtain actionable information?
<--- Score

40. Will there be any necessary staff changes (redundancies or new hires)?
<--- Score

41. What are air emissions accounts?
<--- Score

42. When you map the key players in your own work and the types/domains of relationships with them, which relationships do you find easy and which challenging, and why?
<--- Score

43. Will the energy efficiency retrofit project benefit low income or disadvantaged communities?
<--- Score

44. What does your business emission profile look like?
<--- Score

45. How do an institutions actions interact and fit within the broader energy system?
<--- Score

46. Do you have the right capabilities and capacities?
<--- Score

47. Why will customers want to buy your organizations products/services?
<--- Score

48. What could happen if you do not do it?
<--- Score

49. Were lessons learned captured and communicated?
<--- Score

50. Are the emissions already tracked and reported by another organization?
<--- Score

51. What could be done to help increase natural carbon sinks?
<--- Score

52. Which emission sources should be included in an inventory?
<--- Score

53. Is a GHG Emissions Accounting team work effort in place?
<--- Score

54. What carbon footprinting tools are currently available?
<--- Score

55. Who will be responsible for deciding whether GHG Emissions Accounting goes ahead or not after the initial investigations?
<--- Score

56. How can you incorporate support to ensure safe and effective use of GHG Emissions Accounting into the services that you provide?

<--- Score

57. How is the obligation for emissions valued?
<--- Score

58. Do you engage with organization government suppliers on climate change?
<--- Score

59. What are the implications for review of accounting information if guidance is too generic?
<--- Score

60. Should you address only climate change mitigation or also adaptation?
<--- Score

61. How uncertain information become effective?
<--- Score

62. Which indirect emissions should you report?
<--- Score

63. What are the ingredients of successful travel behavioural change campaigns?
<--- Score

64. How will further internal reductions be achieved in the coming year?
<--- Score

65. Why there is no organizationalization yet?
<--- Score

66. What is carbon management system?
<--- Score

67. Where do you find information on the emissions of the transportation sector as a whole?
<--- Score

68. How can you negotiate GHG Emissions Accounting successfully with a stubborn boss, an irate client, or a deceitful coworker?
<--- Score

69. Can you maintain your growth without detracting from the factors that have contributed to your success?
<--- Score

70. How do you provide a safe environment -physically and emotionally?
<--- Score

71. Do you see more potential in people than they do in themselves?
<--- Score

72. What is a feasible sequencing of reform initiatives over time?
<--- Score

73. Is your basic point ______ or ______?
<--- Score

74. Does the mitigation option really reduce emissions of methane or nitrous oxide?
<--- Score

75. Where do you find default carbon content factors?

<--- Score

76. How does your organization confirm its participation?
<--- Score

77. How do senior leaders deploy your organizations vision and values through your leadership system, to the workforce, to key suppliers and partners, and to customers and other stakeholders, as appropriate?
<--- Score

78. Who are your customers?
<--- Score

79. Does the emission reduction align with other similar projects elsewhere?
<--- Score

80. What model year is your vehicle?
<--- Score

81. Is your strategy driving your strategy? Or is the way in which you allocate resources driving your strategy?
<--- Score

82. What are the status and trends of climate change related indicators and of indicators on how society is affected by climate change and climate change policies?
<--- Score

83. Are resources in place to promote by stakeholders?
<--- Score

84. What else should you disclose about your purchases?
<--- Score

85. Is maximizing GHG Emissions Accounting protection the same as minimizing GHG Emissions Accounting loss?
<--- Score

86. What is consumption based carbon emissions accounting?
<--- Score

87. What should you stop doing?
<--- Score

88. Do you participate in any emissions trading schemes?
<--- Score

89. Is technological change biased toward energy?
<--- Score

90. How should your organization make calculations?
<--- Score

91. What is your strategy for complying with the schemes in which you participate or anticipate participating?
<--- Score

92. Does your organization demonstrate commitment to sustainability?
<--- Score

93. Where should you put your resources?
<--- Score

94. What are specific GHG Emissions Accounting rules to follow?
<--- Score

95. Are there different kinds of greenhouse gas inventories?
<--- Score

96. Are resources available for use?
<--- Score

97. How many days a week do you take public transit to work?
<--- Score

98. Why are air emissions important?
<--- Score

99. What is the craziest thing you can do?
<--- Score

100. Is average daily travel time expenditure constant?
<--- Score

101. What do you do to reduce emissions, and in what order?
<--- Score

102. What are you trying to prove to yourself, and how might it be hijacking your life and business success?
<--- Score

103. What relationships among GHG Emissions Accounting trends do you perceive?
<--- Score

104. What can be meaningfully conveyed to policymakers about the direct benefits of climate policy?
<--- Score

105. Are attitudes important in travel choice?
<--- Score

106. Who will determine interim and final deadlines?
<--- Score

107. What information should you report?
<--- Score

108. Does the scheme have materials with a low embodied energy coefficient and long life expectancy?
<--- Score

109. How do you help reduce greenhouse gases?
<--- Score

110. How do greenhouse gases affect the atmosphere?
<--- Score

111. What are the implications of climate change?
<--- Score

112. In a project to restructure GHG Emissions Accounting outcomes, which stakeholders would you

involve?
<--- Score

113. Why do private companies demand an audit?
<--- Score

114. What are the effects of existing or potential future government regulations in key operating jurisdictions?
<--- Score

115. Is flare combustion reported separately?
<--- Score

116. Where do you find information on estimating emissions from projects with a baseline?
<--- Score

117. When does the carbon cycle begin and end?
<--- Score

118. How and why is the geography of carbon emissions changing?
<--- Score

119. What is sensible to simplify without prejudice to quality?
<--- Score

120. What kind of target should you set?
<--- Score

121. When does organizational investor activism increase shareholder value?
<--- Score

122. Is there any other information which you think your organization should report?
<--- Score

123. How will you insure seamless interoperability of GHG Emissions Accounting moving forward?
<--- Score

124. How will you motivate the stakeholders with the least vested interest?
<--- Score

125. How can energy storage projects actually prove avoided emissions?
<--- Score

126. Can the schedule be done in the given time?
<--- Score

127. How many carbon unit transactions?
<--- Score

128. What constitutes the emerging good practices in accounting for emissions trading schemes?
<--- Score

129. What happens at your organization when people fail?
<--- Score

130. What is the source of the strategies for GHG Emissions Accounting strengthening and reform?
<--- Score

131. Are you changing as fast as the world around you?

<--- Score

132. What are your organizations most important products or services?
<--- Score

133. What information is critical to your organization that your executives are ignoring?
<--- Score

134. Operational - will it work?
<--- Score

135. What are the differences between complete, transitional, basic, and historical reporting?
<--- Score

136. What are the pathways and potentials for reducing emissions from heat and power generation?
<--- Score

137. Is your organizations emissions reduction target realistic?
<--- Score

138. Did your employees make progress today?
<--- Score

139. Do ratings of organization converge?
<--- Score

140. What type of registry system would be the most suitable?
<--- Score

141. Who is responsible for GHG Emissions Accounting?
<--- Score

142. What are your most important goals for the strategic GHG Emissions Accounting objectives?
<--- Score

143. What did you miss in the interview for the worst hire you ever made?
<--- Score

144. Ask yourself: how would you do this work if you only had one staff member to do it?
<--- Score

145. To whom do you add value?
<--- Score

146. How likely is it that a customer would recommend your company to a friend or colleague?
<--- Score

147. Is a high level of uptake possible?
<--- Score

148. Which GHG Emissions Accounting goals are the most important?
<--- Score

149. How is implementation research currently incorporated into each of your goals?
<--- Score

150. What activities are you currently undertaking to reduce emissions organization-wide?

<--- Score

151. Has senior management made climate related or carbon pricing commitments?
<--- Score

152. Why should you adopt a GHG Emissions Accounting framework?
<--- Score

153. Is your organization carbon neutral?
<--- Score

154. What is the likely price level that may be imposed by the government authorities?
<--- Score

155. What is something you believe that nearly no one agrees with you on?
<--- Score

156. What is the likely range of emission reductions from the use of international offsets?
<--- Score

157. Whom among your colleagues do you trust, and for what?
<--- Score

158. Are countries on track to meet climate commitments?
<--- Score

159. What is best for accuracy of emissions?
<--- Score

160. Who is on the team?
<--- Score

161. Is guidance on baselines, projections and benchmarking provided?
<--- Score

162. What are the highest targeted levels of carbon reduction?
<--- Score

163. What policy interventions could encourage changes?
<--- Score

164. What management system can you use to leverage the GHG Emissions Accounting experience, ideas, and concerns of the people closest to the work to be done?
<--- Score

165. What else would be useful to know in order to increase the uptake of low carbon technologies?
<--- Score

166. How do you set GHG Emissions Accounting stretch targets and how do you get people to not only participate in setting these stretch targets but also that they strive to achieve these?
<--- Score

167. What is the relationship between dedicated staff and local leadership?
<--- Score

168. Do you have a flow diagram of what happens?

<--- Score

169. Would you rather sell to knowledgeable and informed customers or to uninformed customers?
<--- Score

170. Is it economical; do you have the time and money?
<--- Score

171. Is the concept of materiality shifting as you move to a carbon constrained economy?
<--- Score

172. Do you get by without bioenergy?
<--- Score

173. Are you using a design thinking approach and integrating Innovation, GHG Emissions Accounting Experience, and Brand Value?
<--- Score

174. What level of accuracy is sufficient for different categories?
<--- Score

175. What are the challenges?
<--- Score

176. Why is carbon accounting important?
<--- Score

177. If you were responsible for initiating and implementing major changes in your organization, what steps might you take to ensure acceptance of those changes?

<--- Score

178. What are its implications for climate policy?
<--- Score

179. How can you become the company that would put you out of business?
<--- Score

180. Does coordinated organizational activism work?
<--- Score

181. Are there demonstrable and measurable carbon reduction benefits arising from the intervention?
<--- Score

182. Who, on the executive team or the board, has spoken to a customer recently?
<--- Score

183. Do you know who is a friend or a foe?
<--- Score

184. Does your organization use an internal price on carbon?
<--- Score

185. Where have emissions trading systems been implemented?
<--- Score

186. What is an unauthorized commitment?
<--- Score

187. Can a conservative estimate be made based on existing information or sources?
<--- Score

188. Do necessary human, legal, administrative, financial and technical resources exist?
<--- Score

189. Who is the main stakeholder, with ultimate responsibility for driving GHG Emissions Accounting forward?
<--- Score

190. Will it be accepted by users?
<--- Score

191. Are countries on track to meet the climate commitments?
<--- Score

192. What type of fuel does your vehicle use?
<--- Score

193. What is the purpose of GHG Emissions Accounting in relation to the mission?
<--- Score

194. Why are you choosing to manage carbon?
<--- Score

195. Are resources in place to widely used currently?
<--- Score

196. Can leak repair logs be used to determine leak duration?

<--- Score

197. Do you feel that more should be done in the GHG Emissions Accounting area?
<--- Score

198. How do you deal with complex organization structures and shared ownership?
<--- Score

199. How do you keep the momentum going?
<--- Score

200. If your customer were your grandmother, would you tell her to buy what you're selling?
<--- Score

201. How do you stay inspired?
<--- Score

202. What do you disclose in your report?
<--- Score

203. What is it like to work for you?
<--- Score

204. How derived is the demand for travel?
<--- Score

205. Who is responsible for errors?
<--- Score

206. Are your responses positive or negative?
<--- Score

207. What stupid rule would you most like to kill?

<--- Score

208. If your company went out of business tomorrow, would anyone who doesn't get a paycheck here care?
<--- Score

209. What is the big GHG Emissions Accounting idea?
<--- Score

210. Should you include avoidance of deforestation in the international response to climate change?
<--- Score

211. Do you have to calculate and report emissions from dry seals?
<--- Score

212. Where does carbon accounting currently stand?
<--- Score

213. Why would a financial organization calculate the carbon footprint of its assets?
<--- Score

214. Does a GHG Emissions Accounting quantification method exist?
<--- Score

215. Does the project involve clearing any land?
<--- Score

216. How do you choose a baseline year?
<--- Score

217. Which emissions/gases are accounted for?
<--- Score

218. What determines reporting behaviour?
<--- Score

219. How many minutes does your commute to work typically take?
<--- Score

220. What metrics can inform and track investor activities, positioning, and signaling?
<--- Score

221. Are resources in place to promote increased uptake?
<--- Score

222. How are forward contracts to purchase/sell emissions allowances accounted for?
<--- Score

223. Is information about environmental and corporate governance matters material?
<--- Score

224. Is the reporter the facility, or all facilities operated by the same organization?
<--- Score

225. What are the benefits for your organization?
<--- Score

226. Do you agree that other organizations should specify an intensity ratio?
<--- Score

227. Do energy audits help reduce barriers to energy efficiency?
<--- Score

228. Is GHG Emissions Accounting dependent on the successful delivery of a current project?
<--- Score

229. Do you forecast your organizations future emissions and/or energy use?
<--- Score

230. Do emission totals appear consistent between facilities based on the magnitude and type of operations?
<--- Score

231. Do GHG Emissions Accounting rules make a reasonable demand on a users capabilities?
<--- Score

232. What would you recommend your friend do if he/she were facing this dilemma?
<--- Score

233. Why would carbon pricing be more effective than other instruments?
<--- Score

234. What amount of greenhouse gas arises from the supply of heat and electricity?
<--- Score

235. Are fuel economy factors by vehicle type available?

<--- Score

236. Have new benefits been realized?
<--- Score

237. Are assumptions made in GHG Emissions Accounting stated explicitly?
<--- Score

238. Do you have a current emissions reduction target?
<--- Score

239. If you got fired and a new hire took your place, what would she do different?
<--- Score

240. How do you cross-sell and up-sell your GHG Emissions Accounting success?
<--- Score

241. How acceptable or unacceptable to you are the various potential climate changes?
<--- Score

242. What are the essentials of internal GHG Emissions Accounting management?
<--- Score

243. Does your organization provide recycling or safe disposal service for products supplied?
<--- Score

244. What are the common emission reduction targets?
<--- Score

245. Is your business prepared to monetize carbon?
<--- Score

246. How do investors use information relating to corporate governance?
<--- Score

247. Can you do all this work?
<--- Score

248. Are all key stakeholders present at all Structured Walkthroughs?
<--- Score

249. What are internal and external GHG Emissions Accounting relations?
<--- Score

250. Who will manage the integration of tools?
<--- Score

251. How will you know that the GHG Emissions Accounting project has been successful?
<--- Score

252. Who else should you help?
<--- Score

253. What are current GHG Emissions Accounting paradigms?
<--- Score

254. How do you make it meaningful in connecting GHG Emissions Accounting with what users do day-

to-day?
<--- Score

255. How you ensure your information is credible?
<--- Score

256. What is good practice and where you can find good practice guidance in the IPCC Guidelines?
<--- Score

257. What co2 target would you choose for humanity?
<--- Score

258. Is climate change integrated into your business strategy?
<--- Score

259. Have emissions increased or decreased?
<--- Score

260. Why is the distinction between direct and indirect emissions important?
<--- Score

261. What determines the quality and credibility of your emissions information?
<--- Score

262. What should a proof of concept or pilot accomplish?
<--- Score

263. Which models, tools and techniques are necessary?
<--- Score

264. How do you compare emissions of different gases?
<--- Score

265. How do you ensure that implementations of GHG Emissions Accounting products are done in a way that ensures safety?
<--- Score

266. What are the associated carbon emissions?
<--- Score

267. How complete is the information provided?
<--- Score

268. What are the effects of climate change?
<--- Score

269. Are new benefits received and understood?
<--- Score

270. Will you do it before the carbon market closes?
<--- Score

271. How many miles do you live from your place of work?
<--- Score

272. What form of price signal is the most appropriate for your organizations situation and its timeframes?
<--- Score

273. What is internal carbon pricing?

<--- Score

274. What aspects of the carbon cycle must be considered in climate policy?
<--- Score

275. Has implementation been effective in reaching specified objectives so far?
<--- Score

276. What are the short and long-term GHG Emissions Accounting goals?
<--- Score

277. Have you been involved in the origination of project based carbon credits?
<--- Score

278. Is the option socially, economically and environmentally sustainable?
<--- Score

279. How prepared is your organization to handle a changing regulatory environment?
<--- Score

280. What actually is a carbon footprint?
<--- Score

281. Are you a full time employee or part time employee?
<--- Score

282. Think of your GHG Emissions Accounting project, what are the main functions?
<--- Score

283. Who do you want your customers to become?
<--- Score

284. What is the significance of carbon sinks in relation to climate change?
<--- Score

285. Do necessary human, legal, administrative, financial, technical resources exist?
<--- Score

286. What percentage of your total operational spend in the reporting year was on energy?
<--- Score

287. How much do you compact it using past knowledge?
<--- Score

288. How should your organization draw boundaries?
<--- Score

289. What are the challenges and benefits associated with providing information on corporate governance and environmental matters?
<--- Score

290. What may be the consequences for the performance of an organization if all stakeholders are not consulted regarding GHG Emissions Accounting?
<--- Score

291. How many days per week do you work?

<--- Score

292. How to assess fairness and ambition?
<--- Score

293. Do you believe that mandated timelines would lead to speedier project completion for most projects?
<--- Score

294. What is the funding source for this project?
<--- Score

295. How can investors set climate related targets using available metrics?
<--- Score

296. Which industry and product is the largest contributor to overall emissions?
<--- Score

297. How do customers see your organization?
<--- Score

298. Is there an associated established platform for reporting?
<--- Score

299. How can an internal carbon pricing system add to the fulfilment of commitments?
<--- Score

300. Do you have past GHG Emissions Accounting successes?
<--- Score

301. What counts that you are not counting?
<--- Score

302. Can existing co2 waste streams meet future productivity demands?
<--- Score

303. What are carbon dioxide removal and negative emissions?
<--- Score

304. What role does communication play in the success or failure of a GHG Emissions Accounting project?
<--- Score

305. How much biofuel do you consume?
<--- Score

306. What is the difference between direct and indirect emissions and what is relevance?
<--- Score

307. Is there any existing GHG Emissions Accounting governance structure?
<--- Score

308. How is your organization positioned for the energy climate transition?
<--- Score

309. Do you agree that your organization should specify which approach it is using to set its organizational boundary?
<--- Score

310. Should quoted companies report all emissions?
<--- Score

311. How much carbon dioxide is produced when different fuels are burned?
<--- Score

312. Why not do GHG Emissions Accounting?
<--- Score

313. Have you purchased any project based carbon credits?
<--- Score

314. Where are purchased allowances recorded on the balance sheet?
<--- Score

315. Are the assumptions believable and achievable?
<--- Score

316. Is the GHG Emissions Accounting organization completing tasks effectively and efficiently?
<--- Score

317. How do you get the community involved in your climate protection effort?
<--- Score

318. Is there an energy efficiency gap?
<--- Score

319. If you weren't already in this business, would you enter it today? And if not, what are you going to do about it?

<--- Score

320. Which of the policy options are supported and why?
<--- Score

321. How do you govern and fulfill your societal responsibilities?
<--- Score

322. How do you foster innovation?
<--- Score

323. Which individuals, teams or departments will be involved in GHG Emissions Accounting?
<--- Score

324. Is there a threshold for emissions reporting?
<--- Score

325. What is the overall business strategy?
<--- Score

326. How do you lead with GHG Emissions Accounting in mind?
<--- Score

327. What are the long-term GHG Emissions Accounting goals?
<--- Score

328. What is the nature of an emission right?
<--- Score

329. Why do other organizations engage in environmental management?

<--- Score

330. Who do you think the world wants your organization to be?
<--- Score

331. How do you deal with GHG Emissions Accounting changes?
<--- Score

332. If you had to rebuild your organization without any traditional competitive advantages (i.e., no killer technology, promising research, innovative product/ service delivery model, etcetera), how would your people have to approach their work and collaborate together in order to create the necessary conditions for success?
<--- Score

333. How do you know if you are successful?
<--- Score

334. What are your personal philosophies regarding GHG Emissions Accounting and how do they influence your work?
<--- Score

335. Who will provide the final approval of GHG Emissions Accounting deliverables?
<--- Score

336. What are the success criteria that will indicate that GHG Emissions Accounting objectives have been met and the benefits delivered?
<--- Score

337. Is there any reason to believe the opposite of my current belief?
<--- Score

338. What about the emergency generator emissions?
<--- Score

Add up total points for this section:
_____ = Total points for this section

Divided by: ______ (number of statements answered) = ______
Average score for this section

Transfer your score to the GHG Emissions Accounting Index at the beginning of the Self-Assessment.

GHG Emissions Accounting and Managing Projects, Criteria for Project Managers:

1.0 Initiating Process Group: GHG Emissions Accounting

1. During which stage of Risk planning are modeling techniques used to determine overall effects of risks on GHG Emissions Accounting project objectives for high probability, high impact risks?

2. If the risk event occurs, what will you do?

3. If action is called for, what form should it take?

4. Are you properly tracking the progress of the GHG Emissions Accounting project and communicating the status to stakeholders?

5. What are the pressing issues of the hour?

6. How will you know you did it?

7. Who is behind the GHG Emissions Accounting project?

8. Are you just doing busywork to pass the time?

9. Were sponsors and decision makers available when needed outside regularly scheduled meetings?

10. What areas does the group agree are the biggest success on the GHG Emissions Accounting project?

11. Were resources available as planned?

12. Specific - is the objective clear in terms of what, how, when, and where the situation will be changed?

13. How should needs be met?

14. Who does what?

15. Are identified risks being monitored properly, are new risks arising during the GHG Emissions Accounting project or are foreseen risks occurring?

16. How is each deliverable reviewed, verified, and validated?

17. The GHG Emissions Accounting project managers have maximum authority in which type of organization?

18. What is the stake of others in your GHG Emissions Accounting project?

19. Will the GHG Emissions Accounting project meet the client requirements, and will it achieve the business success criteria that justified doing the GHG Emissions Accounting project in the first place?

20. How well did the chosen processes fit the needs of the GHG Emissions Accounting project?

1.1 Project Charter: GHG Emissions Accounting

21. What is in it for you?

22. How will you learn more about the process or system you are trying to improve?

23. What barriers do you predict to your success?

24. Why have you chosen the aim you have set forth?

25. Are you building in-house ?

26. Did your GHG Emissions Accounting project ask for this?

27. If finished, on what date did it finish?

28. What are the assumptions?

29. Major high-level milestone targets: what events measure progress?

30. When will this occur?

31. What are some examples of a business case?

32. Why is it important?

33. What is the justification?

34. Name and describe the elements that deal with

providing the detail?

35. What changes can you make to improve?

36. What material?

37. What are you striving to accomplish (measurable goal(s))?

38. What ideas do you have for initial tests of change (PDSA cycles)?

39. Why is a GHG Emissions Accounting project Charter used?

40. Are there special technology requirements?

1.2 Stakeholder Register: GHG Emissions Accounting

41. How will reports be created?

42. How should employers make voices heard?

43. How much influence do they have on the GHG Emissions Accounting project?

44. What opportunities exist to provide communications?

45. Who is managing stakeholder engagement?

46. Who are the stakeholders?

47. What is the power of the stakeholder?

48. What & Why?

49. What are the major GHG Emissions Accounting project milestones requiring communications or providing communications opportunities?

50. How big is the gap?

51. Who wants to talk about Security?

52. Is your organization ready for change?

1.3 Stakeholder Analysis Matrix: GHG Emissions Accounting

53. Who is directly responsible for decisions on issues important to the GHG Emissions Accounting project?

54. What is your Advocacy Strategy?

55. Are you working on the right risks?

56. Participatory approach: how will key stakeholders participate in the GHG Emissions Accounting project?

57. What is the stakeholders name, what is function?

58. Economy - home, abroad?

59. What do you need to appraise?

60. Are the required specifications for products or services changing?

61. Why involve the stakeholder?

62. Disadvantages of proposition?

63. If the baseline is now, and if its improved it will be better than now?

64. Supporters; who are the supporters?

65. Guiding question: who shall you involve in the making of the stakeholder map?

66. Competitors vulnerabilities?

67. What are the key services, contractual arrangements, or other relationships between stakeholder groups?

68. Information and research?

69. What is the stakeholders power and status in relation to the GHG Emissions Accounting project?

70. Who is most dependent on the resources at stake?

71. What unique or lowest-cost resources does the GHG Emissions Accounting project have access to?

72. Who influences whom?

2.0 Planning Process Group: GHG Emissions Accounting

73. Professionals want to know what is expected from them; what are the deliverables?

74. What is the critical path for this GHG Emissions Accounting project, and what is the duration of the critical path?

75. Are there efficient coordination mechanisms to avoid overloading the counterparts, participating stakeholders?

76. Will you be replaced?

77. What is the NEXT thing to do?

78. Is the GHG Emissions Accounting project making progress in helping to achieve the set results?

79. In what way has the GHG Emissions Accounting project come up with innovative measures for problem-solving?

80. Did you read it correctly?

81. Is the duration of the program sufficient to ensure a cycle that will GHG Emissions Accounting project the sustainability of the interventions?

82. Explanation: is what the GHG Emissions Accounting project intents to solve a hard question?

83. Have operating capacities been created and/or reinforced in partners?

84. If a risk event occurs, what will you do?

85. To what extent are the visions and actions of the partners consistent or divergent with regard to the program?

86. Mitigate. what will you do to minimize the impact should a risk event occur?

87. What business situation is being addressed?

88. If task x starts two days late, what is the effect on the GHG Emissions Accounting project end date?

89. Does the program have follow-up mechanisms (to verify the quality of the products, punctuality of delivery, etc.) to measure progress in the achievement of the envisaged results?

90. If a task is partitionable, is this a sufficient condition to reduce the GHG Emissions Accounting project duration?

2.1 Project Management Plan: GHG Emissions Accounting

91. What is GHG Emissions Accounting project scope management?

92. How do you organize the costs in the GHG Emissions Accounting project management plan?

93. How well are you able to manage your risk?

94. Who manages integration?

95. What is risk management?

96. What went wrong?

97. Does the selected plan protect privacy?

98. What does management expect of PMs?

99. Are calculations and results of analyzes essentially correct?

100. How do you manage time?

101. What are the training needs?

102. Is mitigation authorized or recommended?

103. What would you do differently what did not work?

104. What is the business need?

105. What data/reports/tools/etc. do program managers need?

106. Are cost risk analysis methods applied to develop contingencies for the estimated total GHG Emissions Accounting project costs?

107. Is the budget realistic?

108. What should you drop in order to add something new?

109. Are there non-structural buyout or relocation recommendations?

2.2 Scope Management Plan: GHG Emissions Accounting

110. Are changes in scope (deliverable commitments) agreed to by all affected groups & individuals?

111. What are the risks that could significantly affect the schedule of the GHG Emissions Accounting project?

112. What happens if scope changes?

113. Is there a formal set of procedures supporting Stakeholder Management?

114. Time estimation – how much time will be needed?

115. Deliverables -are the deliverables tangible and verifiable?

116. Is it standard practice to formally commit stakeholders to the GHG Emissions Accounting project via agreements?

117. Is current scope of the GHG Emissions Accounting project substantially different than that originally defined?

118. Is there a GHG Emissions Accounting project organization chart showing the reporting relationships and responsibilities for each position?

119. Is there general agreement & acceptance of the current status and progress of the GHG Emissions Accounting project?

120. What strengths do you have?

121. Are the GHG Emissions Accounting project plans updated on a frequent basis?

122. For which criterion is it tolerable not to meet the original parameters?

123. Were GHG Emissions Accounting project team members involved in the development of activity & task decomposition?

124. Do GHG Emissions Accounting project managers participating in the GHG Emissions Accounting project know the GHG Emissions Accounting projects true status first hand?

125. Do you secure formal approval of changes and requirements from stakeholders?

126. Are procurement deliverables arriving on time and to specification?

127. Are target dates established for each milestone deliverable?

128. Are action items captured and managed?

129. Pop quiz – what changed on GHG Emissions Accounting project scope statement input?

2.3 Requirements Management Plan: GHG Emissions Accounting

130. Do you have an agreed upon process for alerting the GHG Emissions Accounting project Manager if a request for change in requirements leads to a product scope change?

131. Will you use an assessment of the GHG Emissions Accounting project environment as a tool to discover risk to the requirements process?

132. What performance metrics will be used?

133. Describe the process for rejecting the GHG Emissions Accounting project requirements. Who has the authority to reject GHG Emissions Accounting project requirements?

134. Is there formal agreement on who has authority to approve a change in requirements?

135. Does the GHG Emissions Accounting project have a Change Control process?

136. Are actual resource expenditures versus planned still acceptable?

137. How knowledgeable is the primary Stakeholder(s) in the proposed application area?

138. Could inaccurate or incomplete requirements in this GHG Emissions Accounting project create a

serious risk for the business?

139. How will the information be distributed?

140. Will the GHG Emissions Accounting project requirements become approved in writing?

141. If it exists, where is it housed?

142. How will bidders price evaluations be done, by deliverables, phases, or in a big bang?

143. Will you use tracing to help understand the impact of a change in requirements?

144. Will you document changes to requirements?

145. Controlling GHG Emissions Accounting project requirements involves monitoring the status of the GHG Emissions Accounting project requirements and managing changes to the requirements. Who is responsible for monitoring and tracking the GHG Emissions Accounting project requirements?

146. Business analysis scope?

147. How will you communicate scheduled tasks to other team members?

148. Will you perform a Requirements Risk assessment and develop a plan to deal with risks?

149. Who will do the reporting and to whom will reports be delivered?

2.4 Requirements Documentation: GHG Emissions Accounting

150. What is the risk associated with the technology?

151. How much does requirements engineering cost?

152. Have the benefits identified with the system being identified clearly?

153. Who provides requirements?

154. Where do you define what is a customer, what are the attributes of customer?

155. What marketing channels do you want to use: e-mail, letter or sms?

156. What are the acceptance criteria?

157. Consistency. are there any requirements conflicts?

158. How does the proposed GHG Emissions Accounting project contribute to the overall objectives of your organization?

159. If applicable; are there issues linked with the fact that this is an offshore GHG Emissions Accounting project?

160. How linear / iterative is your Requirements Gathering process (or will it be)?

161. Do technical resources exist?

162. Is your business case still valid?

163. Who is interacting with the system?

164. What images does it conjure?

165. Is new technology needed?

166. Where do system and software requirements come from, what are sources?

167. Are there legal issues?

168. What facilities must be supported by the system?

169. What are current process problems?

2.5 Requirements Traceability Matrix: GHG Emissions Accounting

170. Will you use a Requirements Traceability Matrix?

171. What are the chronologies, contingencies, consequences, criteria?

172. What is the WBS?

173. Do you have a clear understanding of all subcontracts in place?

174. Is there a requirements traceability process in place?

175. Why use a WBS?

176. How small is small enough?

177. What percentage of GHG Emissions Accounting projects are producing traceability matrices between requirements and other work products?

178. Why do you manage scope?

179. How will it affect the stakeholders personally in career?

180. How do you manage scope?

181. Describe the process for approving requirements so they can be added to the traceability matrix

and GHG Emissions Accounting project work can be performed. Will the GHG Emissions Accounting project requirements become approved in writing?

2.6 Project Scope Statement: GHG Emissions Accounting

182. What went right?

183. Will all GHG Emissions Accounting project issues be unconditionally tracked through the issue resolution process?

184. Will you need a statement of work?

185. If there are vendors, have they signed off on the GHG Emissions Accounting project Plan?

186. Who will you recommend approve the change, and when do you recommend the change reviews occur?

187. Why do you need to manage scope?

188. What process would you recommend for creating the GHG Emissions Accounting project scope statement?

189. Will statistics related to QA be collected, trends analyzed, and problems raised as issues?

190. Will all tasks resulting from issues be entered into the GHG Emissions Accounting project Plan and tracked through the plan?

191. If you were to write a list of what should not be included in the scope statement, what are the things

that you would recommend be described as out-of-scope?

192. Are the meetings set up to have assigned note takers that will add action/issues to the issue list?

193. Will the risk plan be updated on a regular and frequent basis?

194. Will there be a Change Control Process in place?

195. Is the plan for your organization of the GHG Emissions Accounting project resources adequate?

196. Is there a Quality Assurance Plan documented and filed?

197. Will this process be communicated to the customer and GHG Emissions Accounting project team?

198. Was planning completed before the GHG Emissions Accounting project was initiated?

199. Are there specific processes you will use to evaluate and approve/reject changes?

200. Did your GHG Emissions Accounting project ask for this?

2.7 Assumption and Constraint Log: GHG Emissions Accounting

201. Model-building: what data-analytic strategies are useful when building proportional-hazards models?

202. What weaknesses do you have?

203. Were the system requirements formally reviewed prior to initiating the design phase?

204. Security analysis has access to information that is sanitized?

205. Do the requirements meet the standards of correctness, completeness, consistency, accuracy, and readability?

206. What worked well?

207. Are funding and staffing resource estimates sufficiently detailed and documented for use in planning and tracking the GHG Emissions Accounting project?

208. Is the steering committee active in GHG Emissions Accounting project oversight?

209. Is this process still needed?

210. When can log be discarded?

211. Is there documentation of system capability

requirements, data requirements, environment requirements, security requirements, and computer and hardware requirements?

212. Is the definition of the GHG Emissions Accounting project scope clear; what needs to be accomplished?

213. How can constraints be violated?

214. Is this model reasonable?

215. How do you design an auditing system?

216. Are there standards for code development?

217. Does the document/deliverable meet general requirements (for example, statement of work) for all deliverables?

218. Are you meeting your customers expectations consistently?

219. Is there adequate stakeholder participation for the vetting of requirements definition, changes and management?

220. Diagrams and tables are included to account for complex concepts and increase overall readability?

2.8 Work Breakdown Structure: GHG Emissions Accounting

221. When does it have to be done?

222. Can you make it?

223. How many levels?

224. Is the work breakdown structure (wbs) defined and is the scope of the GHG Emissions Accounting project clear with assigned deliverable owners?

225. What has to be done?

226. What is the probability of completing the GHG Emissions Accounting project in less that xx days?

227. Do you need another level?

228. Who has to do it?

229. Is it a change in scope?

230. What is the probability that the GHG Emissions Accounting project duration will exceed xx weeks?

231. How big is a work-package?

232. How much detail?

233. Is it still viable?

234. Where does it take place?

235. Why would you develop a Work Breakdown Structure?

236. When would you develop a Work Breakdown Structure?

237. When do you stop?

2.9 WBS Dictionary: GHG Emissions Accounting

238. Does the contractor use objective results, design reviews and tests to trace schedule performance?

239. Are data being used by managers in an effective manner to ascertain GHG Emissions Accounting project or functional status, to identify reasons or significant variance, and to initiate appropriate corrective action?

240. Is the entire contract planned in time-phased control accounts to the extent practicable?

241. The total budget for the contract (including estimates for authorized and unpriced work)?

242. Are the overhead pools formally and adequately identified?

243. Intermediate schedules, as required, which provide a logical sequence from the master schedule to the control account level?

244. Does the contractors system include procedures for measuring the performance of critical subcontractors?

245. Does the contractors system description or procedures require that the performance measurement baseline plus management reserve equal the contract budget base?

246. Are internal budgets for authorized, and not priced changes based on the contractors resource plan for accomplishing the work?

247. Knowledgeable GHG Emissions Accounting projections of future performance?

248. Are estimates of costs at completion generated in a rational, consistent manner?

249. Are the variances between budgeted and actual indirect costs identified and analyzed at the level of assigned responsibility for control (indirect pool, department, etc.)?

250. Are overhead costs budgets established on a basis consistent with anticipated direct business base?

251. Is the work done on a work package level as described in the WBS dictionary?

252. Changes in the current direct and GHG Emissions Accounting projected base?

253. Are time-phased budgets established for planning and control of level of effort activity by category of resource; for example, type of manpower and/or material?

254. Are there procedures for monitoring action items and corrective actions to the point of resolution and are corresponding procedures being followed?

255. Are overhead cost budgets established for each

organization which has authority to incur overhead costs?

256. Are indirect costs accumulated for comparison with the corresponding budgets?

2.10 Schedule Management Plan: GHG Emissions Accounting

257. Are all activities logically sequenced?

258. Have all unresolved risks been documented?

259. Are the constraints or deadlines associated with the task accurate?

260. Do all stakeholders know how to access this repository and where to find the GHG Emissions Accounting project documentation?

261. Is documentation created for communication with the suppliers and Vendors?

262. Are written status reports provided on a designated frequent basis?

263. Have GHG Emissions Accounting project success criteria been defined?

264. Will rolling way planning be used?

265. Does the schedule have reasonable float?

266. Have stakeholder accountabilities & responsibilities been clearly defined?

267. Has the schedule been baselined?

268. Has a provision been made to reassess GHG

Emissions Accounting project risks at various GHG Emissions Accounting project stages?

269. Who is responsible for estimating the activity durations?

270. Have GHG Emissions Accounting project management standards and procedures been identified / established and documented?

271. Is the development plan and/or process documented?

272. Are any non-compliance issues that exist due to your organizations practices communicated to your organization?

273. Are non-critical path items updated and agreed upon with the teams?

274. Does the GHG Emissions Accounting project have quality set of schedule BOEs?

275. What date will the task finish?

276. Has your organization readiness assessment been conducted?

2.11 Activity List: GHG Emissions Accounting

277. How detailed should a GHG Emissions Accounting project get?

278. What did not go as well?

279. Should you include sub-activities?

280. Is there anything planned that does not need to be here?

281. How should ongoing costs be monitored to try to keep the GHG Emissions Accounting project within budget?

282. How will it be performed?

283. What are you counting on?

284. Can you determine the activity that must finish, before this activity can start?

285. What is the LF and LS for each activity?

286. What will be performed?

287. In what sequence?

288. What is your organizations history in doing similar activities?

289. How can the GHG Emissions Accounting project be displayed graphically to better visualize the activities?

290. What went well?

291. Who will perform the work?

292. Are the required resources available or need to be acquired?

293. The wbs is developed as part of a joint planning session. and how do you know that youhave done this right?

294. When do the individual activities need to start and finish?

2.12 Activity Attributes: GHG Emissions Accounting

295. Where else does it apply?

296. How difficult will it be to do specific activities on this GHG Emissions Accounting project?

297. Are the required resources available?

298. Activity: what is Missing?

299. Resources to accomplish the work?

300. What activity do you think you should spend the most time on?

301. Resource is assigned to?

302. How much activity detail is required?

303. Does your organization of the data change its meaning?

304. How else could the items be grouped?

305. Can more resources be added?

306. Have you identified the Activity Leveling Priority code value on each activity?

307. Do you feel very comfortable with your prediction?

308. Have constraints been applied to the start and finish milestones for the phases?

309. Activity: fair or not fair?

310. Is there a trend during the year?

311. What is missing?

2.13 Milestone List: GHG Emissions Accounting

312. How soon can the activity finish?

313. How will the milestone be verified?

314. It is to be a narrative text providing the crucial aspects of your GHG Emissions Accounting project proposal answering what, who, how, when and where?

315. How late can the activity start?

316. When will the GHG Emissions Accounting project be complete?

317. Which path is the critical path?

318. Describe your organizations strengths and core competencies. What factors will make your organization succeed?

319. New USPs?

320. Calculate how long can activity be delayed?

321. Reliability of data, plan predictability?

322. Obstacles faced?

323. Insurmountable weaknesses?

324. Do you foresee any technical risks or developmental challenges?

325. What would happen if a delivery of material was one week late?

326. Sustainable financial backing?

327. Describe the concept of the technology, product or service that will be or has been developed. How will it be used?

328. What are your competitors vulnerabilities?

329. Identify critical paths (one or more) and which activities are on the critical path?

2.14 Network Diagram: GHG Emissions Accounting

330. Which type of network diagram allows you to depict four types of dependencies?

331. How confident can you be in your milestone dates and the delivery date?

332. If a current contract exists, can you provide the vendor name, contract start, and contract expiration date?

333. What job or jobs follow it?

334. What activity must be completed immediately before this activity can start?

335. What is the completion time?

336. Exercise: what is the probability that the GHG Emissions Accounting project duration will exceed xx weeks?

337. Review the logical flow of the network diagram. Take a look at which activities you have first and then sequence the activities. Do they make sense?

338. What controls the start and finish of a job?

339. Planning: who, how long, what to do?

340. Why must you schedule milestones, such as

reviews, throughout the GHG Emissions Accounting project?

341. What to do and When?

342. If the GHG Emissions Accounting project network diagram cannot change and you have extra personnel resources, what is the BEST thing to do?

343. Where do you schedule uncertainty time?

344. What is the lowest cost to complete this GHG Emissions Accounting project in xx weeks?

345. What are the tools?

346. Where do schedules come from?

2.15 Activity Resource Requirements: GHG Emissions Accounting

347. How many signatures do you require on a check and does this match what is in your policy and procedures?

348. Other support in specific areas?

349. Are there unresolved issues that need to be addressed?

350. Do you use tools like decomposition and rolling-wave planning to produce the activity list and other outputs?

351. What are constraints that you might find during the Human Resource Planning process?

352. Why do you do that?

353. Which logical relationship does the PDM use most often?

354. What is the Work Plan Standard?

355. How do you handle petty cash?

356. Organizational Applicability?

357. Time for overtime?

358. Anything else?

359. When does monitoring begin?

2.16 Resource Breakdown Structure: GHG Emissions Accounting

360. What is the purpose of assigning and documenting responsibility?

361. Which resource planning tool provides information on resource responsibility and accountability?

362. How difficult will it be to do specific activities on this GHG Emissions Accounting project?

363. Who needs what information?

364. When do they need the information?

365. Which resources should be in the resource pool?

366. What is the difference between % Complete and % work?

367. What are the requirements for resource data?

368. Why do you do it?

369. Is predictive resource analysis being done?

370. What can you do to improve productivity?

371. Who delivers the information?

372. What is each stakeholders desired outcome for

the GHG Emissions Accounting project?

373. What is GHG Emissions Accounting project communication management?

374. Who will use the system?

375. What is the number one predictor of a groups productivity?

376. What defines a successful GHG Emissions Accounting project?

377. What defines a successful GHG Emissions Accounting project?

2.17 Activity Duration Estimates: GHG Emissions Accounting

378. What is the difference between using brainstorming and the Delphi technique for risk identification?

379. What is wrong with this scenario?

380. How does GHG Emissions Accounting project integration management relate to the GHG Emissions Accounting project life cycle, stakeholders, and the other GHG Emissions Accounting project management knowledge areas?

381. Is a formal written notice that the contract is complete provided to the seller?

382. Are GHG Emissions Accounting project records organized, maintained, and assessable by GHG Emissions Accounting project team members?

383. Which includes asking team members about the time estimates for activities and reaching agreement on the calendar date for each activity?

384. Are GHG Emissions Accounting project results verified and GHG Emissions Accounting project documents archived?

385. What are two suggestions for ensuring adequate change control on GHG Emissions Accounting projects that involve outside contracts?

386. How difficult will it be to do specific activities on this GHG Emissions Accounting project?

387. Which does one need in order to complete schedule development?

388. Describe GHG Emissions Accounting project integration management in your own words. How does GHG Emissions Accounting project integration management relate to the GHG Emissions Accounting project life cycle, stakeholders, and the other GHG Emissions Accounting project management knowledge areas?

389. What type of information goes in a quality assurance plan?

390. Could it have been avoided?

391. Which is correct?

392. Based on , if you need to shorten the duration of the GHG Emissions Accounting project, what activity would you try to shorten?

393. Explanation notice how many choices are half right?

394. Are risks that are likely to affect the GHG Emissions Accounting project identified and documented?

395. Why is outsourcing growing so rapidly?

396. Calculate the expected duration for an activity

that has a most likely time of 3, a pessimistic time of 10, and a optimiztic time of 2?

2.18 Duration Estimating Worksheet: GHG Emissions Accounting

397. How should ongoing costs be monitored to try to keep the GHG Emissions Accounting project within budget?

398. Done before proceeding with this activity or what can be done concurrently?

399. When does your organization expect to be able to complete it?

400. What utility impacts are there?

401. Define the work as completely as possible. What work will be included in the GHG Emissions Accounting project?

402. What work will be included in the GHG Emissions Accounting project?

403. Is a construction detail attached (to aid in explanation)?

404. When, then?

405. What is the total time required to complete the GHG Emissions Accounting project if no delays occur?

406. Will the GHG Emissions Accounting project collaborate with the local community and leverage resources?

407. What questions do you have?

408. Why estimate costs?

409. What is your role?

410. What is cost and GHG Emissions Accounting project cost management?

411. What info is needed?

412. Do any colleagues have experience with your organization and/or RFPs?

413. Is this operation cost effective?

2.19 Project Schedule: GHG Emissions Accounting

414. How detailed should a GHG Emissions Accounting project get?

415. Month GHG Emissions Accounting project take?

416. Why do you need to manage GHG Emissions Accounting project Risk?

417. What does that mean?

418. Are procedures defined by which the GHG Emissions Accounting project schedule may be changed?

419. How closely did the initial GHG Emissions Accounting project Schedule compare with the actual schedule?

420. Why do you need schedules?

421. How can slack be negative?

422. How effectively were issues able to be resolved without impacting the GHG Emissions Accounting project Schedule or Budget?

423. What is risk?

424. Is infrastructure setup part of your GHG Emissions Accounting project?

425. Is there a Schedule Management Plan that establishes the criteria and activities for developing, monitoring and controlling the GHG Emissions Accounting project schedule?

426. How much slack is available in the GHG Emissions Accounting project?

427. Was the GHG Emissions Accounting project schedule reviewed by all stakeholders and formally accepted?

428. What is the difference?

429. Did the GHG Emissions Accounting project come in on schedule?

430. How can you shorten the schedule?

2.20 Cost Management Plan: GHG Emissions Accounting

431. Are key risk mitigation strategies added to the GHG Emissions Accounting project schedule?

432. Have key stakeholders been identified?

433. Is a payment system in place with proper reviews and approvals?

434. Change types and category - What are the types of changes and what are the techniques to report and control changes?

435. Environmental management - what changes in statutory environmental compliance requirements are anticipated during the GHG Emissions Accounting project?

436. Are metrics used to evaluate and manage Vendors?

437. Are the people assigned to the GHG Emissions Accounting project sufficiently qualified?

438. Are risk oriented checklists used during risk identification?

439. Are GHG Emissions Accounting project team members committed fulltime?

440. What is the work breakdown structure for the

GHG Emissions Accounting project?

441. Weve met your goals?

442. Is there a requirements change management processes in place?

443. Is the communication plan being followed?

444. Forecasts – how will the cost to complete the GHG Emissions Accounting project be forecast?

445. Cost / benefit analysis?

446. Progress measurement and control – How will the GHG Emissions Accounting project measure and control progress?

447. Does the detailed work plan match the complexity of tasks with the capabilities of personnel?

448. How do you manage cost?

2.21 Activity Cost Estimates: GHG Emissions Accounting

449. Did the GHG Emissions Accounting project team have the right skills?

450. If you are asked to lower your estimate because the price is too high, what are your options?

451. What makes a good activity description?

452. Scope statement only direct or indirect costs as well?

453. Which contract type places the most risk on the seller?

454. What is your organizations history in doing similar tasks?

455. Were the tasks or work products prepared by the consultant useful?

456. What do you want to know about the stay to know if costs were inappropriately high or low?

457. Who determines the quality and expertise of contractors?

458. Was it performed on time?

459. How do you treat administrative costs in the activity inventory?

460. Review – what are some common errors in activities to avoid?

461. What skill level is required to do the job?

462. One way to define activities is to consider how organization employees describe jobs to families and friends. You basically want to know, What do you do?

463. What defines a successful GHG Emissions Accounting project?

464. Maintenance Reserve?

465. In which phase of the acquisition process cycle does source qualifications reside?

466. Certification of actual expenditures?

467. Vac -variance at completion, how much over/ under budget do you expect to be?

2.22 Cost Estimating Worksheet: GHG Emissions Accounting

468. What additional GHG Emissions Accounting project(s) could be initiated as a result of this GHG Emissions Accounting project?

469. How will the results be shared and to whom?

470. Will the GHG Emissions Accounting project collaborate with the local community and leverage resources?

471. What costs are to be estimated?

472. What is the purpose of estimating?

473. What will others want?

474. What happens to any remaining funds not used?

475. Who is best positioned to know and assist in identifying corresponding factors?

476. Value pocket identification & quantification what are value pockets?

477. Does the GHG Emissions Accounting project provide innovative ways for stakeholders to overcome obstacles or deliver better outcomes?

478. Is the GHG Emissions Accounting project responsive to community need?

479. What can be included?

480. Ask: are others positioned to know, are others credible, and will others cooperate?

481. Is it feasible to establish a control group arrangement?

482. Can a trend be established from historical performance data on the selected measure and are the criteria for using trend analysis or forecasting methods met?

483. Identify the timeframe necessary to monitor progress and collect data to determine how the selected measure has changed?

484. What is the estimated labor cost today based upon this information?

2.23 Cost Baseline: GHG Emissions Accounting

485. What deliverables come first?

486. Will the GHG Emissions Accounting project fail if the change request is not executed?

487. On time?

488. Why do you manage cost?

489. What is cost and GHG Emissions Accounting project cost management?

490. If you sold 10x widgets on a day, what would the affect on profits be?

491. Have you identified skills that are missing from your team?

492. What is it ?

493. On budget?

494. Have all approved changes to the schedule baseline been identified and impact on the GHG Emissions Accounting project documented?

495. Are there contingencies or conditions related to the acceptance?

496. What is the most important thing to do next

to make your GHG Emissions Accounting project successful?

497. Does the suggested change request represent a desired enhancement to the products functionality?

498. GHG Emissions Accounting project goals -should others be reconsidered?

499. Is the cr within GHG Emissions Accounting project scope?

500. Where do changes come from?

501. Have all approved changes to the cost baseline been identified and impact on the GHG Emissions Accounting project documented?

2.24 Quality Management Plan: GHG Emissions Accounting

502. What are your key performance measures/ indicators for tracking progress relative to your action plans?

503. How does your organization make it easy for customers to seek assistance or complain?

504. Meet how often?

505. Who is responsible for writing the qapp?

506. How do you ensure that your sampling methods and procedures meet your data needs?

507. No superfluous information or marketing narrative?

508. Who is responsible?

509. What is the audience for the data?

510. Are there trends or hot spots?

511. How does training support what is important to your organization and the individual?

512. How are calibration records kept?

513. How does your organization manage training and evaluate its effectiveness?

514. How do you field-modify testing procedures?

515. Have GHG Emissions Accounting project management standards and procedures been established and documented?

516. What other teams / processes would be impacted by changes to the current process, and how?

517. How does the material compare to a regulatory threshold?

518. Is there a Quality Management Plan?

519. Sampling part of task?

520. What field records are generated?

521. Can you perform this task or activity in a more effective manner?

2.25 Quality Metrics: GHG Emissions Accounting

522. Did evaluation start on time?

523. Is there a set of procedures to capture, analyze and act on quality metrics?

524. What do you measure?

525. How are requirements conflicts resolved?

526. Filter visualizations of interest?

527. Who notifies stakeholders of normal and abnormal results?

528. Have alternatives been defined in the event that failure occurs?

529. How should customers provide input?

530. What metrics do you measure?

531. Is a risk containment plan in place?

532. Where did complaints, returns and warranty claims come from?

533. Has it met internal or external standards?

534. Are quality metrics defined?

535. Do you stratify metrics by product or site?

536. Have risk areas been identified?

537. Can visual measures help you to filter visualizations of interest?

538. What documentation is required?

539. Product Availability ?

540. What group is empowered to define quality requirements?

541. Which data do others need in one place to target areas of improvement?

2.26 Process Improvement Plan: GHG Emissions Accounting

542. Has a process guide to collect the data been developed?

543. What personnel are the coaches for your initiative?

544. What personnel are the sponsors for that initiative?

545. Does explicit definition of the measures exist?

546. Who should prepare the process improvement action plan?

547. What actions are needed to address the problems and achieve the goals?

548. Are you making progress on your improvement plan?

549. What is the return on investment?

550. What personnel are the champions for the initiative?

551. To elicit goal statements, do you ask a question such as, What do you want to achieve?

552. Does your process ensure quality?

553. How do you measure?

554. Management commitment at all levels?

555. Modeling current processes is great, and will you ever see a return on that investment?

556. What lessons have you learned so far?

557. Have the supporting tools been developed or acquired?

558. Have the frequency of collection and the points in the process where measurements will be made been determined?

559. Are there forms and procedures to collect and record the data?

560. If a process improvement framework is being used, which elements will help the problems and goals listed?

561. What is the test-cycle concept?

2.27 Responsibility Assignment Matrix: GHG Emissions Accounting

562. What will the work cost?

563. The staff interests – is the group or the person interested in working for this GHG Emissions Accounting project?

564. Identify and isolate causes of favorable and unfavorable cost and schedule variances?

565. Most people let you know when others re too busy, and are others really too busy?

566. Are detailed work packages planned as far in advance as practicable?

567. Are authorized changes being incorporated in a timely manner?

568. Do work packages consist of discrete tasks which are adequately described?

569. Is every signing-off responsibility and every communicating responsibility critically necessary?

570. Are records maintained to show how undistributed budgets are controlled?

571. Does the scheduling system identify in a timely manner the status of work?

572. What are the deliverables?

573. Are people encouraged to bring up issues?

574. Direct labor dollars and/or hours?

575. Changes in the nature of the overhead requirements?

576. Are there any drawbacks to using a responsibility assignment matrix?

577. Budgeted cost for work scheduled?

578. What tool can show you individual and group allocations?

2.28 Roles and Responsibilities: GHG Emissions Accounting

579. What expectations were NOT met?

580. What is working well?

581. What areas of supervision are challenging for you?

582. To decide whether to use a quality measurement, ask how will you know when it is achieved?

583. Concern: where are you limited or have no authority, where you can not influence?

584. Are your policies supportive of a culture of quality data?

585. Be specific; avoid generalities. Thank you and great work alone are insufficient. What exactly do you appreciate and why?

586. What areas would you highlight for changes or improvements?

587. Are governance roles and responsibilities documented?

588. Influence: what areas of organizational decision making are you able to influence when you do not have authority to make the final decision?

589. Are the quality assurance functions and related roles and responsibilities clearly defined?

590. Accountabilities: what are the roles and responsibilities of individual team members?

591. What specific behaviors did you observe?

592. Do the values and practices inherent in the culture of your organization foster or hinder the process?

593. What should you do now to prepare for your career 5+ years from now?

594. Once the responsibilities are defined for the GHG Emissions Accounting project, have the deliverables, roles and responsibilities been clearly communicated to every participant?

595. Are your budgets supportive of a culture of quality data?

596. Required skills, knowledge, experience?

597. What should you do now to ensure that you are meeting all expectations of your current position?

598. Is the data complete?

2.29 Human Resource Management Plan: GHG Emissions Accounting

599. Are schedule deliverables actually delivered?

600. Is the schedule updated on a periodic basis?

601. Who is involved?

602. Are tasks tracked by hours?

603. How are you going to ensure that you have a well motivated workforce?

604. What talent is needed?

605. Are trade-offs between accepting the risk and mitigating the risk identified?

606. Was your organizations estimating methodology being used and followed?

607. Have all involved GHG Emissions Accounting project stakeholders and work groups committed to the GHG Emissions Accounting project?

608. Were decisions made in a timely manner?

609. Is the manpower level sufficient to meet the future business requirements?

610. Are changes in deliverable commitments agreed to by all affected groups & individuals?

611. Have adequate resources been provided by management to ensure GHG Emissions Accounting project success?

612. Are key risk mitigation strategies added to the GHG Emissions Accounting project schedule?

613. Responsiveness to change and the resulting demands for different skills and abilities?

2.30 Communications Management Plan: GHG Emissions Accounting

614. Is the stakeholder role recognized by your organization?

615. What is the political influence?

616. Why do you manage communications?

617. Which team member will work with each stakeholder?

618. How did the term stakeholder originate?

619. Do you prepare stakeholder engagement plans?

620. Are the stakeholders getting the information others need, are others consulted, are concerns addressed?

621. How were corresponding initiatives successful?

622. Are others needed?

623. What to learn?

624. Which stakeholders are thought leaders, influences, or early adopters?

625. What does the stakeholder need from the team?

626. Are you constantly rushing from meeting to

meeting?

627. What are the interrelationships?

628. What data is going to be required?

629. What communications method?

630. Which stakeholders can influence others?

631. What is the stakeholders level of authority?

632. In your work, how much time is spent on stakeholder identification?

633. Are there common objectives between the team and the stakeholder?

2.31 Risk Management Plan: GHG Emissions Accounting

634. Do requirements put excessive performance constraints on the product?

635. Premium on reliability of product?

636. What will drive change?

637. Why might it be late?

638. How can you fix it?

639. Are there new risks that mitigation strategies might introduce?

640. What can you do to minimize the impact if it does?

641. For software; are compilers and code generators available and suitable for the product to be built?

642. What other risks are created by choosing an avoidance strategy?

643. Why do you need to manage GHG Emissions Accounting project Risk?

644. How do you manage GHG Emissions Accounting project Risk?

645. Are some people working on multiple GHG

Emissions Accounting projects?

646. Are team members trained in the use of the tools?

647. How are risk analvsis and prioritization performed?

648. Minimize cost and financial risk?

649. How quickly does this item need to be resolved?

650. Have staff received necessary training?

651. Are tools for analysis and design available?

652. How would you suggest monitoring for risk transition indicators?

653. Can the GHG Emissions Accounting project proceed without assuming the risk?

2.32 Risk Register: GHG Emissions Accounting

654. Having taken action, how did the responses effect change, and where is the GHG Emissions Accounting project now?

655. Financial risk -can your organization afford to undertake the GHG Emissions Accounting project?

656. How are risks identified?

657. What is your current and future risk profile?

658. People risk -are people with appropriate skills available to help complete the GHG Emissions Accounting project?

659. Recovery actions - planned actions taken once a risk has occurred to allow you to move on. What should you do after?

660. Are implemented controls working as others should?

661. Assume the event happens, what is the Most Likely impact?

662. Preventative actions - planned actions to reduce the likelihood a risk will occur and/or reduce the seriousness should it occur. What should you do now?

663. Does the evidence highlight any areas to

advance opportunities or foster good relations. If yes what steps will be taken?

664. What is the reason for current performance gaps and do the risks and opportunities identified previously account for this?

665. What is the probability and impact of the risk occurring?

666. How could corresponding Risk affect the GHG Emissions Accounting project in terms of cost and schedule?

667. What is a Risk?

668. Why would you develop a risk register?

669. Risk documentation: what reporting formats and processes will be used for risk management activities?

670. Are corrective measures implemented as planned?

671. Schedule impact/severity estimated range (workdays) assume the event happens, what is the potential impact?

672. What may happen or not go according to plan?

2.33 Probability and Impact Assessment: GHG Emissions Accounting

673. What are the current demands of the customer?

674. Costs associated with late delivery or a defective product?

675. Which functions, departments, and activities of your organization are going to be affected?

676. Are the risk data complete?

677. Who will be responsible for a slippage?

678. Are end-users enthusiastically committed to the GHG Emissions Accounting project and the system/ product to be built?

679. What is the GHG Emissions Accounting project managers level of commitment and professionalism?

680. Has the need for the GHG Emissions Accounting project been properly established?

681. Do you have a mechanism for managing change?

682. How is risk handled within this GHG Emissions Accounting project organization?

683. How do risks change during the GHG Emissions Accounting projects life cycle?

684. Who are the international/overseas GHG Emissions Accounting project partners (equipment supplier/supplier/consultant/contractor) for this GHG Emissions Accounting project?

685. What risks does your organization have if the GHG Emissions Accounting projects fail to meet deadline?

686. What action do you usually take against risks?

687. Supply/demand GHG Emissions Accounting projections and trends; what are the levels of accuracy?

688. To what extent is the chosen technology maturing?

689. What should be the gestation period for the GHG Emissions Accounting project with specific technology?

2.34 Probability and Impact Matrix: GHG Emissions Accounting

690. Are enough people available?

691. Which role do you have in the GHG Emissions Accounting project?

692. Which should be probably done NEXT?

693. Will there be an increase in the political conservatism?

694. Does the customer understand the software process?

695. What is the level of commitment and professionalism?

696. Can you handle the investment risk?

697. Have customers been involved fully in the definition of requirements?

698. How are the local factors going to affect the absorption?

699. What is your anticipated volatility of the requirements?

700. Several experts are offsite, and wish to be included. How can this be done?

701. How likely is the current plan to come in on schedule or on budget?

702. Who has experience with this?

703. Is security a central objective?

704. Why do you need to manage GHG Emissions Accounting project Risk?

705. What is the risk appetite?

706. Which risks need to move on to Perform Quantitative Risk Analysis?

707. Do you have a consistent repeatable process that is actually used?

2.35 Risk Data Sheet: GHG Emissions Accounting

708. What do people affected think about the need for, and practicality of preventive measures?

709. Whom do you serve (customers)?

710. Potential for recurrence?

711. How reliable is the data source?

712. What are you weak at and therefore need to do better?

713. Is the data sufficiently specified in terms of the type of failure being analyzed, and its frequency or probability?

714. How can hazards be reduced?

715. What is the chance that it will happen?

716. Will revised controls lead to tolerable risk levels?

717. What do you know?

718. Has a sensitivity analysis been carried out?

719. Type of risk identified?

720. Risk of what?

721. How do you handle product safely?

722. What are the main opportunities available to you that you should grab while you can?

723. Who has a vested interest in how you perform as your organization (our stakeholders)?

724. What were the Causes that contributed?

725. During work activities could hazards exist?

726. What will be the consequences if it happens?

2.36 Procurement Management Plan: GHG Emissions Accounting

727. Does the GHG Emissions Accounting project team have the right skills?

728. Are post milestone GHG Emissions Accounting project reviews (PMPR) conducted with your organization at least once a year?

729. Sensitivity analysis?

730. Has a resource management plan been created?

731. Were GHG Emissions Accounting project team members involved in detailed estimating and scheduling?

732. Have external dependencies been captured in the schedule?

733. Have GHG Emissions Accounting project team accountabilities & responsibilities been clearly defined?

734. Are vendor invoices audited for accuracy before payment?

735. Are software metrics formally captured, analyzed and used as a basis for other GHG Emissions Accounting project estimates?

736. Staffing Requirements?

737. Are cause and effect determined for risks when others occur?

738. Is there a procurement management plan in place?

739. Have adequate resources been provided by management to ensure GHG Emissions Accounting project success?

2.37 Source Selection Criteria: GHG Emissions Accounting

740. What should be considered?

741. What is cost analysis and when should it be performed?

742. Do you want to wait until all offerors have been evaluated?

743. Do proposed hours support content and schedule?

744. Have team members been adequately trained?

745. What common questions or problems are associated with debriefings?

746. Do you prepare an independent cost estimate?

747. What benefits are accrued from issuing a DRFP in advance of issuing a final RFP?

748. What are the requirements for publicizing a RFP?

749. Team leads: what is your process for assigning ratings?

750. Are they compliant with all technical requirements?

751. Will the technical evaluation factor unnecessarily

force the acquisition into a higher-priced market segment?

752. How do you ensure an integrated assessment of proposals?

753. What evidence should be provided regarding proposal evaluations?

754. If the costs are normalized, please account for how the normalization is conducted. Is a cost realism analysis used?

755. How much past performance information should be requested?

756. What are the most critical evaluation criteria that prove to be tiebreakers in the evaluation of proposals?

757. Does your documentation identify why the team concurs or differs with reported performance from past performance report (CPARs, questionnaire responses, etc.)?

758. Are types/quantities of material, facilities appropriate?

2.38 Stakeholder Management Plan: GHG Emissions Accounting

759. Is it standard practice to formally commit stakeholders to the GHG Emissions Accounting project via agreements?

760. What is meant by managing the triple constraint?

761. Have all stakeholders been identified?

762. Which of the records created within the GHG Emissions Accounting project, if any, does the Business Owner require access to?

763. Does the system design reflect the requirements?

764. Are formal code reviews conducted?

765. Are there cosmetic errors that hinder readability and comprehension?

766. Do GHG Emissions Accounting project managers participating in the GHG Emissions Accounting project know the GHG Emissions Accounting projects true status first hand?

767. Is there a Steering Committee in place?

768. How many GHG Emissions Accounting project staff does this specific process affect?

769. Are GHG Emissions Accounting project team

members involved in detailed estimating and scheduling?

770. What procedures will be utilised to ensure effective monitoring of GHG Emissions Accounting project progress?

771. Are mitigation strategies identified?

772. Are internal GHG Emissions Accounting project status meetings held at reasonable intervals?

773. Are corrective actions and variances reported?

774. Does the GHG Emissions Accounting project have a Quality Culture?

2.39 Change Management Plan: GHG Emissions Accounting

775. Where will the funds come from?

776. What tasks are needed?

777. Why is the initiative is being undertaken - What are the business drivers?

778. What is going to be done differently?

779. Different application of an existing process?

780. What provokes organizational change?

781. What is the negative impact of communicating too soon or too late?

782. What is the worst thing that can happen if you chose not to communicate this information?

783. Who will fund the training?

784. How will you deal with anger about the restricting of communications due to confidentiality considerations?

785. What are the key change management success metrics?

786. What do you expect the target audience to do, say, think or feel as a result of this communication?

787. Has the training provider been established?

788. Is there a software application relevant to this deliverable?

789. When does it make sense to customize?

790. What relationships will change?

791. What method and medium would you use to announce a message?

792. What would be an estimate of the total cost for the activities required to carry out the change initiative?

793. Do you need new systems?

3.0 Executing Process Group: GHG Emissions Accounting

794. What type of people would you want on your team?

795. How do you enter durations, link tasks, and view critical path information?

796. What are the typical GHG Emissions Accounting project management skills?

797. What are the GHG Emissions Accounting project management deliverables of each process group?

798. What is the shortest possible time it will take to complete this GHG Emissions Accounting project?

799. What is involved in the solicitation process?

800. How does the job market and current state of the economy affect human resource management?

801. How can software assist in GHG Emissions Accounting project communications?

802. In what way has the program come up with innovative measures for problem-solving?

803. Will outside resources be needed to help?

804. Contingency planning. if a risk event occurs, what will you do?

805. How can software assist in procuring goods and services?

806. What were things that you did well, and could improve, and how?

807. How will professionals learn what is expected from them what the deliverables are?

808. How can you use Microsoft GHG Emissions Accounting project and Excel to assist in GHG Emissions Accounting project risk management?

809. What areas were overlooked on this GHG Emissions Accounting project?

810. What are crucial elements of successful GHG Emissions Accounting project plan execution?

811. Who will provide training?

812. What areas does the group agree are the biggest success on the GHG Emissions Accounting project?

3.1 Team Member Status Report: GHG Emissions Accounting

813. How it is to be done?

814. How does this product, good, or service meet the needs of the GHG Emissions Accounting project and your organization as a whole?

815. Does your organization have the means (staff, money, contract, etc.) to produce or to acquire the product, good, or service?

816. How will resource planning be done?

817. Are the attitudes of staff regarding GHG Emissions Accounting project work improving?

818. How much risk is involved?

819. Is there evidence that staff is taking a more professional approach toward management of your organizations GHG Emissions Accounting projects?

820. Does the product, good, or service already exist within your organization?

821. The problem with Reward & Recognition Programs is that the truly deserving people all too often get left out. How can you make it practical?

822. Does every department have to have a GHG Emissions Accounting project Manager on staff?

823. Why is it to be done?

824. What is to be done?

825. What specific interest groups do you have in place?

826. How can you make it practical?

827. Will the staff do training or is that done by a third party?

828. Are your organizations GHG Emissions Accounting projects more successful over time?

829. Are the products of your organizations GHG Emissions Accounting projects meeting customers objectives?

830. Do you have an Enterprise GHG Emissions Accounting project Management Office (EPMO)?

831. When a teams productivity and success depend on collaboration and the efficient flow of information, what generally fails them?

3.2 Change Request: GHG Emissions Accounting

832. Why do you want to have a change control system?

833. Who needs to approve change requests?

834. Who will perform the change?

835. What kind of information about the change request needs to be captured?

836. Does the schedule include GHG Emissions Accounting project management time and change request analysis time?

837. What has an inspector to inspect and to check?

838. How are the measures for carrying out the change established?

839. How well do experienced software developers predict software change?

840. How to get changes (code) out in a timely manner?

841. Will this change conflict with other requirements changes (e.g., lead to conflicting operational scenarios)?

842. Has a formal technical review been conducted to

assess technical correctness?

843. For which areas does this operating procedure apply?

844. How is the change documented (format, content, storage)?

845. Who is responsible for the implementation and monitoring of all measures?

846. Should staff call into the helpdesk or go to the website?

847. Who can suggest changes?

848. What are the requirements for urgent changes?

849. How many lines of code must be changed to implement the change?

3.3 Change Log: GHG Emissions Accounting

850. When was the request approved?

851. Is the change request open, closed or pending?

852. Is the change backward compatible without limitations?

853. When was the request submitted?

854. Is the change request within GHG Emissions Accounting project scope?

855. How does this relate to the standards developed for specific business processes?

856. Does the suggested change request seem to represent a necessary enhancement to the product?

857. Is the requested change request a result of changes in other GHG Emissions Accounting project(s)?

858. Do the described changes impact on the integrity or security of the system?

859. Is the submitted change a new change or a modification of a previously approved change?

860. Will the GHG Emissions Accounting project fail if the change request is not executed?

861. Who initiated the change request?

862. How does this change affect scope?

863. Should a more thorough impact analysis be conducted?

864. Is this a mandatory replacement?

865. How does this change affect the timeline of the schedule?

3.4 Decision Log: GHG Emissions Accounting

866. Who is the decisionmaker?

867. What makes you different or better than others companies selling the same thing?

868. It becomes critical to track and periodically revisit both operational effectiveness; Are you noticing all that you need to, and are you interpreting what you see effectively?

869. What is the average size of your matters in an applicable measurement?

870. Is your opponent open to a non-traditional workflow, or will it likely challenge anything you do?

871. Adversarial environment. is your opponent open to a non-traditional workflow, or will it likely challenge anything you do?

872. How does provision of information, both in terms of content and presentation, influence acceptance of alternative strategies?

873. Who will be given a copy of this document and where will it be kept?

874. How do you know when you are achieving it?

875. Which variables make a critical difference?

876. What is your overall strategy for quality control / quality assurance procedures?

877. What was the rationale for the decision?

878. What eDiscovery problem or issue did your organization set out to fix or make better?

879. Does anything need to be adjusted?

880. What alternatives/risks were considered?

881. Do strategies and tactics aimed at less than full control reduce the costs of management or simply shift the cost burden?

882. Is everything working as expected?

883. How consolidated and comprehensive a story can you tell by capturing currently available incident data in a central location and through a log of key decisions during an incident?

884. How effective is maintaining the log at facilitating organizational learning?

885. Meeting purpose; why does this team meet?

3.5 Quality Audit: GHG Emissions Accounting

886. Have the risks associated with the intentions been identified, analyzed and appropriate responses developed?

887. How does your organization know that its system for supporting staff research capability is appropriately effective and constructive?

888. Are the intentions consistent with external obligations (such as applicable laws)?

889. Do the acceptance procedures and specifications include the criteria for acceptance/rejection, define the process to be used, and specify the measuring and test equipment that is to be used?

890. Does the audit organization have experience in performing the required work for entities of your type and size?

891. How well do you think your organization engages with the outside community?

892. How does your organization know that its management of its ethical responsibilities is appropriately effective and constructive?

893. How does your organization know that its research planning and management systems are appropriately effective and constructive in enabling

quality research outcomes?

894. What does an analysis of your organizations staff profile suggest in terms of its planning, and how is this being addressed?

895. Is there a risk that information provided by management may not always be reliable?

896. How does your organization know that the quality of its supervisors is appropriately effective and constructive?

897. How does your organization know that its system for recruiting the best staff possible are appropriately effective and constructive?

898. How does your organization know that its system for commercializing research outputs is appropriately effective and constructive?

899. How does your organization know that the support for its staff is appropriately effective and constructive?

900. Is there any content that may be legally actionable?

901. How does your organization know that its quality of teaching is appropriately effective and constructive?

902. How does your organization know that it provides a safe and healthy environment?

903. How does your organization know that its public

relations and marketing systems are appropriately effective and constructive?

904. How does your organization know that its systems for assisting staff with career planning and employment placements are appropriately effective and constructive?

905. Statements of intent remain exactly that until they are put into effect. The next step is to deploy the already stated intentions. In other words, do the plans happen in reality?

3.6 Team Directory: GHG Emissions Accounting

906. Process decisions: do job conditions warrant additional actions to collect job information and document on-site activity?

907. How does the team resolve conflicts and ensure tasks are completed?

908. Contract requirements complied with?

909. Who will be the stakeholders on your next GHG Emissions Accounting project?

910. Decisions: what could be done better to improve the quality of the constructed product?

911. When will you produce deliverables?

912. Decisions: is the most suitable form of contract being used?

913. Who will write the meeting minutes and distribute?

914. When does information need to be distributed?

915. Days from the time the issue is identified?

916. How do unidentified risks impact the outcome of the GHG Emissions Accounting project?

917. Who are the Team Members?

918. Where should the information be distributed?

919. Process decisions: how well was task order work performed?

920. Process decisions: is work progressing on schedule and per contract requirements?

921. Why is the work necessary?

922. How and in what format should information be presented?

923. Process decisions: are contractors adequately prosecuting the work?

924. Who will talk to the customer?

925. Do purchase specifications and configurations match requirements?

3.7 Team Operating Agreement: GHG Emissions Accounting

926. Do team members reside in more than two countries?

927. Do you ensure that all participants know how to use the required technology?

928. Must your team members rely on the expertise of other members to complete tasks?

929. Are team roles clearly defined and accepted?

930. Do you post meeting notes and the recording (if used) and notify participants?

931. What are the safety issues/risks that need to be addressed and/or that the team needs to consider?

932. Communication protocols: how will the team communicate?

933. What is the number of cases currently teamed?

934. Are there more than two functional areas represented by your team?

935. Are there more than two native languages represented by your team?

936. Do team members need to frequently communicate as a full group to make timely

decisions?

937. Do you brief absent members after they view meeting notes or listen to a recording?

938. Did you delegate tasks such as taking meeting minutes, presenting a topic and soliciting input?

939. To whom do you deliver your services?

940. Are there differences in access to communication and collaboration technology based on team member location?

941. Do you vary your voice pace, tone and pitch to engage participants and gain involvement?

942. What are the current caseload numbers in the unit?

943. What individual strengths does each team member bring to the group?

3.8 Team Performance Assessment: GHG Emissions Accounting

944. To what degree are the teams goals and objectives clear, simple, and measurable?

945. What makes opportunities more or less obvious?

946. To what degree can team members vigorously define the teams purpose in considerations with others who are not part of the functioning team?

947. To what degree are the goals ambitious?

948. To what degree are fresh input and perspectives systematically caught and added (for example, through information and analysis, new members, and senior sponsors)?

949. Do you give group members authority to make at least some important decisions?

950. To what degree are the members clear on what they are individually responsible for and what they are jointly responsible for?

951. When a reviewer complains about method variance, what is the essence of the complaint?

952. Is there a particular method of data analysis that you would recommend as a means of demonstrating that method variance is not of great concern for a given dataset?

953. How much interpersonal friction is there in your team?

954. To what degree can team members frequently and easily communicate with one another?

955. To what degree are sub-teams possible or necessary?

956. How do you recognize and praise members for contributions?

957. How hard did you try to make a good selection?

958. To what degree are the goals realistic?

959. Effects of crew composition on crew performance: Does the whole equal the sum of its parts?

960. Where to from here?

961. What are teams?

962. If you have criticized someones work for method variance in your role as reviewer, what was the circumstance?

3.9 Team Member Performance Assessment: GHG Emissions Accounting

963. To what degree do team members feel that the purpose of the team is important, if not exciting?

964. To what degree do the goals specify concrete team work products?

965. What makes them effective?

966. How should adaptive assessments be implemented?

967. To what degree can team members meet frequently enough to accomplish the teams ends?

968. What is needed for effective data teams?

969. To what degree do team members articulate the teams work approach?

970. Who receives a benchmark visit?

971. What are the basic principles and objectives of performance measurement and assessment?

972. To what degree does the teams purpose contain themes that are particularly meaningful and memorable?

973. What are top priorities?

974. To what degree do team members understand one anothers roles and skills?

975. What variables that affect team members achievement are within your control?

976. What innovations (if any) are developed to realize goals?

977. Which training platform formats (i.e., mobile, virtual, videogame-based) were implemented in your effort(s)?

978. Are there any safeguards to prevent intentional or unintentional rating errors?

979. Are any governance changes sufficient to impact achievement?

980. What is used as a basis for instructional decisions?

3.10 Issue Log: GHG Emissions Accounting

981. Is access to the Issue Log controlled?

982. In classifying stakeholders, which approach to do so are you using?

983. Who were proponents/opponents?

984. What is a change?

985. Who have you worked with in past, similar initiatives?

986. Can you think of other people who might have concerns or interests?

987. What are the stakeholders interrelationships?

988. How is this initiative related to other portfolios, programs, or GHG Emissions Accounting projects?

989. Are stakeholder roles recognized by your organization?

990. What effort will a change need?

991. How do you manage human resources?

992. Who reported the issue?

993. Do you feel more overwhelmed by stakeholders?

994. Are they needed?

995. What would have to change?

996. Is there an important stakeholder who is actively opposed and will not receive messages?

997. Who needs to know and how much?

998. What help do you and your team need from the stakeholders?

4.0 Monitoring and Controlling Process Group: GHG Emissions Accounting

999. Is the program making progress in helping to achieve the set results?

1000. How can you monitor progress?

1001. How well did the chosen processes fit the needs of the GHG Emissions Accounting project?

1002. Is the program in place as intended?

1003. How will staff learn how to use the deliverables?

1004. User: who wants the information and what are they interested in?

1005. What do they need to know about the GHG Emissions Accounting project?

1006. Is progress on outcomes due to your program?

1007. How can you make your needs known?

1008. Measurable - are the targets measurable?

1009. What resources are necessary?

1010. How is agile program management done?

1011. Is there sufficient time allotted between the

general system design and the detailed system design phases?

1012. Is it what was agreed upon?

1013. What are the goals of the program?

4.1 Project Performance Report: GHG Emissions Accounting

1014. To what degree does the teams purpose constitute a broader, deeper aspiration than just accomplishing short-term goals?

1015. To what degree do the structures of the formal organization motivate taskrelevant behavior and facilitate task completion?

1016. How will procurement be coordinated with other GHG Emissions Accounting project aspects, such as scheduling and performance reporting?

1017. To what degree do individual skills and abilities match task demands?

1018. To what degree does the formal organization make use of individual resources and meet individual needs?

1019. To what degree will team members, individually and collectively, commit time to help themselves and others learn and develop skills?

1020. To what degree does the funding match the requirement?

1021. To what degree do members articulate the goals beyond the team membership?

1022. To what degree will the team adopt a concrete,

clearly understood, and agreed-upon approach that will result in achievement of the teams goals?

1023. Next Steps?

1024. To what degree does the information network communicate information relevant to the task?

1025. To what degree are the skill areas critical to team performance present?

1026. To what degree can the team ensure that all members are individually and jointly accountable for the teams purpose, goals, approach, and work-products?

1027. To what degree does the teams work approach provide opportunity for members to engage in open interaction?

4.2 Variance Analysis: GHG Emissions Accounting

1028. Are overhead costs budgets established on a basis consistent with the anticipated direct business base?

1029. What is the incurrence of actual indirect costs in excess of budgets, by element of expense?

1030. Contemplated overhead expenditure for each period based on the best information currently is available?

1031. When, during the last four quarters, did a primary business event occur causing a fluctuation?

1032. Is there a logical explanation for any variance?

1033. Historical experience?

1034. Can the contractor substantiate work package and planning package budgets?

1035. Are there quarterly budgets with quarterly performance comparisons?

1036. What can be the cause of an increase in costs?

1037. Did an existing competitor change strategy?

1038. How does the monthly budget compare to the actual experience?

1039. What business event causes fluctuations?

1040. Is data disseminated to the contractors management timely, accurate, and usable?

1041. Budgeted cost for work performed?

1042. Are the bases and rates for allocating costs from each indirect pool consistently applied?

1043. Are all authorized tasks assigned to identified organizational elements?

1044. What should management do?

4.3 Earned Value Status: GHG Emissions Accounting

1045. When is it going to finish?

1046. How does this compare with other GHG Emissions Accounting projects?

1047. Validation is a process of ensuring that the developed system will actually achieve the stakeholders desired outcomes; Are you building the right product? What do you validate?

1048. Verification is a process of ensuring that the developed system satisfies the stakeholders agreements and specifications; Are you building the product right? What do you verify?

1049. Earned value can be used in almost any GHG Emissions Accounting project situation and in almost any GHG Emissions Accounting project environment. it may be used on large GHG Emissions Accounting projects, medium sized GHG Emissions Accounting projects, tiny GHG Emissions Accounting projects (in cut-down form), complex and simple GHG Emissions Accounting projects and in any market sector. some people, of course, know all about earned value, they have used it for years - but perhaps not as effectively as they could have?

1050. Are you hitting your GHG Emissions Accounting projects targets?

1051. How much is it going to cost by the finish?

1052. Where are your problem areas?

1053. If earned value management (EVM) is so good in determining the true status of a GHG Emissions Accounting project and GHG Emissions Accounting project its completion, why is it that hardly any one uses it in information systems related GHG Emissions Accounting projects?

1054. What is the unit of forecast value?

1055. Where is evidence-based earned value in your organization reported?

4.4 Risk Audit: GHG Emissions Accounting

1056. What are the risks that could stop you from achieving your objectives?

1057. Is your organization willing to commit significant time to the requirements gathering process?

1058. For paid staff, does your organization comply with the minimum conditions for employment and/or the applicable modern award?

1059. Is all expenditure authorised through an identified process?

1060. Do you have financial policies and procedures in place to guide officers of your organization/treasurer/general members?

1061. Does the customer have a solid idea of what is required?

1062. How do you govern assets?

1063. Are regular safety inspections made of buildings, grounds and equipment?

1064. Are auditors able to effectively apply more soft evidence found in the risk-assessment process with the results of more tangible audit evidence found through more substantive testing?

1065. Has an event time line been developed?

1066. Do all coaches/instructors/leaders have appropriate and current accreditation?

1067. When your organization is entering into a major contract, does it seek legal advice?

1068. Has everyone (staff, volunteers and participants) agreed to a code of behaviour or conduct?

1069. To what extent are auditors effective at linking business risks and management assertions?

1070. What impact does experience with one client have on decisions made for other clients during the risk-assessment process?

1071. How are risk appetites expressed?

1072. Are you meeting your legal, regulatory and compliance requirements - if not, why not?

1073. What are the strategic implications with clients when auditors focus audit resources based on business-level risks?

1074. What are the commonly used work arounds in high risk areas?

4.5 Contractor Status Report: GHG Emissions Accounting

1075. What process manages the contracts?

1076. What are the minimum and optimal bandwidth requirements for the proposed solution?

1077. What was the overall budget or estimated cost?

1078. What was the actual budget or estimated cost for your organizations services?

1079. What was the budget or estimated cost for your organizations services?

1080. What is the average response time for answering a support call?

1081. Are there contractual transfer concerns?

1082. Who can list a GHG Emissions Accounting project as organization experience, your organization or a previous employee of your organization?

1083. What was the final actual cost?

1084. How is risk transferred?

1085. How does the proposed individual meet each requirement?

1086. How long have you been using the services?

1087. Describe how often regular updates are made to the proposed solution. Are corresponding regular updates included in the standard maintenance plan?

1088. If applicable; describe your standard schedule for new software version releases. Are new software version releases included in the standard maintenance plan?

4.6 Formal Acceptance: GHG Emissions Accounting

1089. Was the GHG Emissions Accounting project goal achieved?

1090. Do you perform formal acceptance or burn-in tests?

1091. What function(s) does it fill or meet?

1092. Does it do what GHG Emissions Accounting project team said it would?

1093. Who would use it?

1094. Did the GHG Emissions Accounting project manager and team act in a professional and ethical manner?

1095. What lessons were learned about your GHG Emissions Accounting project management methodology?

1096. Have all comments been addressed?

1097. Was the GHG Emissions Accounting project work done on time, within budget, and according to specification?

1098. What was done right?

1099. How well did the team follow the methodology?

1100. How does your team plan to obtain formal acceptance on your GHG Emissions Accounting project?

1101. Was the sponsor/customer satisfied?

1102. Who supplies data?

1103. What is the Acceptance Management Process?

1104. Does it do what client said it would?

1105. What can you do better next time?

1106. What features, practices, and processes proved to be strengths or weaknesses?

1107. What are the requirements against which to test, Who will execute?

1108. Did the GHG Emissions Accounting project achieve its MOV?

5.0 Closing Process Group: GHG Emissions Accounting

1109. What communication items need improvement?

1110. What were the desired outcomes?

1111. How well did the team follow the chosen processes?

1112. What will you do?

1113. When will the GHG Emissions Accounting project be done?

1114. Did the delivered product meet the specified requirements and goals of the GHG Emissions Accounting project?

1115. How well did the chosen processes produce the expected results?

1116. Can the lesson learned be replicated?

1117. Will the GHG Emissions Accounting project deliverable(s) replace a current asset or group of assets?

1118. Did the GHG Emissions Accounting project team have the right skills?

1119. What is the risk of failure to your organization?

1120. Is this an updated GHG Emissions Accounting project Proposal Document?

1121. How critical is the GHG Emissions Accounting project success to the success of your organization?

1122. What is the GHG Emissions Accounting project Management Process?

1123. What areas were overlooked on this GHG Emissions Accounting project?

5.1 Procurement Audit: GHG Emissions Accounting

1124. Is there a formal program of inservice training for personnel in the business management function?

1125. Are procurement policies and practices in line with (international) good practice standards?

1126. Is the opportunity properly published?

1127. Is the foreseen budget compared with similar GHG Emissions Accounting projects or procurements yet realised (historical standards)?

1128. Were calculations used in evaluation adequate and correct?

1129. Can changes be made to automatic disbursement programs without proper approval of management?

1130. Does your organization have an administrative timetable to assist the staff in implementing the budget calendar?

1131. Is each copy of the purchase order necessary?

1132. Could the bidders assess the economic risks the successful bidder would be responsible for, thus limiting the inclusion of extra charges for risk?

1133. Is the procurement process organized the

most appropriate way taking into consideration the amount of procurement?

1134. Is funding made available for payments under the contract at the appropriate time and in accordance with the relevant national/public financial procedures?

1135. Are incentives to deliver on time and in quantity properly specified?

1136. Is data securely stored?

1137. Is a cost/benefit analysis, a cost/effectiveness or a financial analysis considering life-cycle costs performed and is the funding of the procurement guaranteed?

1138. Did the contracting authority verify compliance with the basic requirements of the competition?

1139. Are the number of checking accounts where cash segregation is not required kept to a reasonable number?

1140. Is the weighting set coherent, convincing and leaving little scope for arbitrary and random evaluation and ranking?

1141. Is the accounting distribution of expenses included with the request for payment?

1142. Does the procurement function/unit have the ability to negotiate with customers and suppliers?

1143. Was there a sound basis for the scorings applied

to the criteria and was the scoring well balanced?

5.2 Contract Close-Out: GHG Emissions Accounting

1144. Have all contract records been included in the GHG Emissions Accounting project archives?

1145. Are the signers the authorized officials?

1146. Why Outsource?

1147. Parties: Authorized?

1148. Was the contract complete without requiring numerous changes and revisions?

1149. Have all contracts been completed?

1150. How/when used ?

1151. Has each contract been audited to verify acceptance and delivery?

1152. Was the contract type appropriate?

1153. How does it work?

1154. How is the contracting office notified of the automatic contract close-out?

1155. Change in circumstances?

1156. Have all contracts been closed?

1157. Change in knowledge?

1158. Change in attitude or behavior?

1159. Was the contract sufficiently clear so as not to result in numerous disputes and misunderstandings?

1160. What is capture management?

1161. Parties: who is involved?

1162. Have all acceptance criteria been met prior to final payment to contractors?

1163. What happens to the recipient of services?

5.3 Project or Phase Close-Out: GHG Emissions Accounting

1164. Who are the GHG Emissions Accounting project stakeholders and what are roles and involvement?

1165. Did the delivered product meet the specified requirements and goals of the GHG Emissions Accounting project?

1166. What advantages do the an individual interview have over a group meeting, and vice-versa?

1167. What were the goals and objectives of the communications strategy for the GHG Emissions Accounting project?

1168. What are the marketing communication needs for each stakeholder?

1169. What is the information level of detail required for each stakeholder?

1170. What was expected from each stakeholder?

1171. What stakeholder group needs, expectations, and interests are being met by the GHG Emissions Accounting project?

1172. What is this stakeholder expecting?

1173. What hierarchical authority does the stakeholder have in your organization?

1174. Does the lesson educate others to improve performance?

1175. Complete yes or no?

1176. Who exerted influence that has positively affected or negatively impacted the GHG Emissions Accounting project?

1177. When and how were information needs best met?

1178. Have business partners been involved extensively, and what data was required for them?

1179. Who controlled key decisions that were made?

1180. Were risks identified and mitigated?

5.4 Lessons Learned: GHG Emissions Accounting

1181. Were the aims and objectives achieved?

1182. How smooth do you feel Integration has been?

1183. What was helpful to know when planning the deployment?

1184. How was the GHG Emissions Accounting project controlled?

1185. What is your working hypothesis, if you have one?

1186. How accurately and timely was the Risk Management Log updated or reviewed?

1187. What should have been accomplished during predeployment that was not accomplished?

1188. What were the most significant issues on this GHG Emissions Accounting project?

1189. Was the control overhead justified?

1190. How was the quality of products/processes assured?

1191. What were the success factors?

1192. Is there any way in which you think your

development process hampered this GHG Emissions Accounting project?

1193. What is the growth stage of your organization?

1194. What mistakes did you successfully avoid making?

1195. Overall, how effective were the efforts to prepare you and your organization for the impact of the product/service of the GHG Emissions Accounting project?

1196. How much communication is socially oriented?

1197. What needs to be done over or differently?

1198. What specialization does the task require?

1199. What things mattered the most on this GHG Emissions Accounting project?

Index